ROUTLEDGE LIBRARY EDITIONS:
BUSINESS AND ECONOMICS IN ASIA

Volume 3

ASIAN AND UNITED STATES MARKET REACTIONS TO TRADE RESTRICTIONS

ASIAN AND UNITED STATES MARKET REACTIONS TO TRADE RESTRICTIONS

QIAN SUN

Routledge
Taylor & Francis Group

LONDON AND NEW YORK

First published in 1996 by Garland Publishing, Inc.

This edition first published in 2019
by Routledge
2 Park Square, Milton Park, Abingdon, Oxon OX14 4RN

and by Routledge
52 Vanderbilt Avenue, New York, NY 10017

Routledge is an imprint of the Taylor & Francis Group, an informa business

© 1996 Qian Sun

British Library Cataloguing in Publication Data
A catalogue record for this book is available from the British Library

ISBN: 978-1-138-48274-6 (Set)
ISBN: 978-0-429-42825-8 (Set) (ebk)
ISBN: 978-1-138-31281-4 (Volume 3) (hbk)
ISBN: 978-0-429-45800-2 (Volume 3) (ebk)

Publisher's Note
The publisher has gone to great lengths to ensure the quality of this reprint but points out that some imperfections in the original copies may be apparent.

Disclaimer
The publisher has made every effort to trace copyright holders and would welcome correspondence from those they have been unable to trace.

ASIAN AND UNITED STATES MARKET REACTIONS TO TRADE RESTRICTIONS

QIAN SUN

GARLAND PUBLISHING, Inc.
New York & London / 1996

Library of Congress Cataloging-in-Publication Data

Sun, Qian, 1956–
  Asian and United States market reactions to trade restric-
tions / Qian Sun.
      p.   cm. — (Financial sector of the American economy)
  Revision of the author's thesis (Ph.D.—Arizona State Univer-
sity, 1991).
  Includes bibliographical references and index.
  ISBN 0-8153-2626-2 (alk. paper)
  1. Protectionism—United States. 2. Balance of trade—United
States. 3. Stocks—Prices—United States. 4. Stocks—Prices—
Taiwan. 5. Stocks—Prices—Korea, South. I. Title. II. Series.
HF1756.S83 1996
382'.5'0973—dc20   96-36693

Printed on acid-free, 250-year-life paper
Manufactured in the United States of America

To my parents

Contents

List Of Tables

List Of Figures

Foreword

The effect of U.S. protectionist policy on stock prices of firms in the U.S. and abroad is still an open question. In theory, the effects are ambiguous. While common intuition may suggest that greater U.S. trade restrictions will harm foreign firms that export to the U.S. market and benefit U.S. firms, such effects need not occur. Models exist that suggest protectionist policy may increase profits and prices of both domestic and foreign firms when goods are substitutes in oligopolistic markets. As a result of the theoretical ambiguities, the issue of stock price effects of trade restrictions is an empirical question. Evidence like that presented in the following pages is required to understand the real-world dynamics.

An investigation of the effects of trade restrictions must be executed at the level of the individual firm. Previous researchers have explored the sensitivity of U.S. firm values to trade restrictions but have not examined the effects on foreign firms. A major contribution of this paper is to extend the analysis to its sensible next step: what are the effects on individual foreign firms? In recent years, the availability of firm-level data for foreign markets allows such an analysis. By focusing on Asian firms that export to the United States, the study focuses on a region that has concerned U.S. policymakers due to the apparent comparative advantage that resides in that region for a broad category of manufactured goods. Specifically, the analysis of Asian industries that have been involved in trade disputes with their U.S. counterparts, provides a strong test of the effects of trade restrictions on stock prices.

As with all event-type studies in finance, issues of dating the arrival of information are important. For instance, if the U.S. International Trade Commission announces that U.S. producers have been injured by Asian television manufacturers, one expects that Asian TV exporters will find their stock prices falling with the announcement. In the particular case of televisions, Korean firms had negative abnormal returns associated with the announcement of damage to U.S. firms and alleged dumping by the Korean firms. Several months following the initial announcement of damage, the Korean firms were able to successfully document that their home-market prices were lower than originally thought. The announcement that penalties were being reduced was associated with positive abnormal returns.

This book is a gold mine of information regarding episodes like the one just discussed. Only through careful analysis of the data, using appropriate statistical techniques, can we expect to learn how trade protectionism affects stock prices. Such analysis is of interest to investors and portfolio managers seeking to understand the dynamic adjustment of stock prices of multinational firms around trade conflict events. Beyond the investment dimension, the analysis in this text has also a pure scholarly contribution. Rather than rely on assertion by politicians or involved parties to understand who gets hurt in trade protection disputes, we can instead turn to the impartial view of the equity markets to gain independent evidence regarding the benefits and costs of trade protectionism. Qian Sun has given us a book that provides needed evidence on one of the major policy isues of our time.

Michael Melvin
May 1996

Preface

The purpose of this book is to examine the possible impact of U.S. trade restrictions and trade deficit news on stock prices of U.S. import-competing and Korean and Taiwanese export-oriented firms. The persistently large U.S. merchandise trade deficit has sparked off a series of U.S. trade conflicts trade restrictions with its trading partners These events have been hot topics among academics, the general public, and policy makers. The topics are hot because they have wide implications to trade-related firms, the general public, and international relations. Many authors have studied the impact of the trade deficit and trade restrictions from a macroeconomic perspective, i.e., the impact on employment rate, national income, consumer welfare, etc.. This book tries to measure the impact at the firm and/or industry level. It is well known that a stock's price reflects the public's expectation of the firm's future cash flows and their associated risks. Any new information that affects this expectation will affect the stock price. According to market efficiency hypotheses, if trade restriction and trade deficit news contain such information, it should be immediately reflected in the firm's stock price. By examining the impact on stock prices, this book can shed some lights on the following two issues. First, do trade restrictions benefit the U.S. import-competing firms and hurt foreign export-oriented firms? The empirical evidence on this issue has a direct implication on the effectiveness of the trade restrictions. Second, does the trade deficit news signal an increased probability of imposing trade restrictions or a further loss of competitiveness of U.S. import-competing firms? The empirical evidence on this issue shows how the market reads the trade deficit news.

Several authors have investigated the impact of trade deficit and trade restriction news on stock prices. However, they mainly focus on the U.S. market. The previous examinations of the trade deficit news effect on stock prices were only limited to stock market indices. This book distinguishes from the existing trade news literature in three aspects. First, by extending the trade related news study to foreign markets, specifically to Korean and Taiwanese export-oriented firms, this book provides some evidence on whether U.S. trade restriction and trade deficit news affect some foreign markets more than they do the U.S. market. This possibility is based on the theory that a small open economy gains more from free trade than a large open economy. However, when trade conflicts arise, the small open economy loses more than the large open economy because the large open economy's market is much more valuable to the small open economy than is the opposite. Both the Korean and Taiwanese economies are small relative to the U.S. economy and their fast growth is heavily reliant on the exports to the U.S.. Second, by examining stock prices at both the market and firm levels, this book tries to distinguish between the possible signals conveyed by the trade deficit news, and also reduce the watering down effect resulting from focusing on market indices alone. Third, by using Korean and Taiwanese data, this book can better test both the hypothesis that the trade deficit news signals an increasing probability of raising protection and the competing hypothesis that the trade deficit news signals the further deteriorating competitiveness of U.S. import-competing firms. Since both the Korean and Taiwanese currencies were pegged to the U.S. dollar for most of the 1980s, the complicated trade deficit effect on stock prices via exchange rate change can, to a great extent, be avoided.

It is really a pleasure to publish this book with the Garland Publishing, Inc. as part of the series, *The Financial Sector of the American Economy*. This book represents a revision of my doctoral dissertation completed at Arizona State University in 1991. Changes have been made in almost every chapter. In chapter 2, the literature review is updated to acknowledge the more recent scholarship in this area. In order to increase the power of the test, the original event study methodology described in chapter 3 is replaced by the more recent version advocated by Dodd and Warner. Consequently, the empirical tests using event studies are updated in chapter 4. The empirical studies on the trade restriction effect on Korean and Taiwanese TV firms are revised in chapter 5 and 6. The conclusion in chapter 7 is also slightly modified. Despite these changes, the main content of this book still remains the same.

My debt to Professor Michael Melvin, my dissertation committee chair, can be warmly acknowledged but never fully recompensed. Without his guidance and support, this book would never have come about. I am also grateful to my committee members, Professors Josef Brada, Roger Faith, Dennis Hoffman, Jose Mendez, and Don Schlagenhauf, for their advice and help. Finally, I would like to thank my colleagues at the Nanyang Business School for their comments and support.

Asian and United States Market Reactions to Trade Restrictions

I

Introduction

The decade of 1970 witnessed a reduction in the competitiveness of corporate America in the world market. They lost market share to Japan, Europe, as well as Newly Industrialized Countries (NICs). The growing U.S. merchandise trade deficit caught the concern of business, U.S. politicians, and the general public.

This trend continued in the 1980s. The entire 1980s was characterized by persistent and large U.S. merchandise trade deficits as is shown in Table 1.1.

In 1987, the U.S. trade deficit reached its peak at $152 billion and the trade deficit as a percentage of GNP also reached its highest at 3.36%. As a consequence, protectionist sentiment reached a new height. Complaints about the unfair trade practices of foreign competitors often hit the headlines and the cases investigated by the United States International Trade Commission (ITC) increased dramatically. The import related cases, such as anti-dumping, counter-veiling, escape clause, market order, and unfair trade practices, were more than doubled in 1980 compared to 1979.[1] On January 11, 1982, seven U.S. steel companies shipped trucks of documents to the ITC and simultaneously filed 93 petitions complaining about foreign competitors.[2] In addition, many bills had been introduced into Congress aimed at protecting domestic industries from foreign competition. Trade conflicts arose not only between the U.S. and Japan and Europe but also between the U.S. and the NICs. Taiwan, South Korea, Brazil, Mexico, Hong Kong and Singapore were often mentioned by the U.S. as so-called "unfair trading partners".

Table 1.1

The U.S. Trade Balance and Its Ratio to GNP ($ in Billion)

	Import	Export	Deficit	GNP	DEF/GNP
1980	245.26	225.72	19.54	2732.0	0.72%
1981	260.98	238.69	22.29	3052.6	0.73%
1982	243.95	216.44	27.51	3166.0	0.87%
1983	258.05	205.64	52.41	3405.7	1.54%
1984	330.68	224.00	106.68	3774.5	2.83%
1985	336.54	218.83	117.71	4014.9	2.93%
1986	365.44	227.16	138.28	4240.3	3.26%
1987	406.24	254.12	152.12	4526.7	3.36%
1988	441.57	321.81	119.76	4889.6	2.45%
1989	477.38	361.46	115.92	5248.2	2.21%

Data Sources: *Foreign Trade Statistics* (1989), Department of Commerce; *International Financial Statistics Yearbook* (1986, 1992), United Nation.

The Reagan administration which covered most of the 1980s and was generally recognized as carrying out a *laissez faire* economic policy, fell short to extend this policy to foreign trade. Pearson (1989) pointed out in his assessment of the Reagan administration's foreign trade policy that the policy displayed a ready acceptance of departures away from liberal trade toward protection based on "political" or pragmatic considerations.

During the period 1981-1988, seven escape clause cases[3] with positive ITC recommendation for protection reached President Reagan and five out of the seven (71 percent) were granted increased protection by the President. During the same period, the Reagan administration had been involved in nine cases where a major domestic industry sought increased protection by appealing directly to Congress, or by engineering foreign "voluntary" export restraint (VER) agreements. These industries were automobiles, nonrubber footwear, textiles and apparel, sugar, machine tools, steel, softwood lumber, copper, and semiconductors. The combined 1987 import value for these industries exceeded $100 billion. Except footwear and copper, all the other industries received additional protection. The Reagan administration was also a vigorous champion of Section 301[4], which gives the U.S. president the authority to remove foreign "unfair" trade practices by unilateral U.S. action so that U.S. exports can be expanded. Between September, 1985 and June, 1988, the U.S. challenged foreign practices 26 times by expediting, initiating or threatening to initiate Section 301 investigations.

In view of the importance of the U.S. market to the world economy, the increased protectionist sentiment in the U.S. and consequently the increased U.S. trade restrictions and U.S.-foreign trade conflicts should have some impact on the U.S. and foreign economies, especially on the sectors related to the U.S. foreign trade. Many studies have been devoted to this area. Most of these studies focused on the impact of the U.S. merchandise trade deficit and trade restrictions on U.S. employment, consumer welfare, and national income.[5] However, based on market efficiency and rational expectation assumptions, if the monthly U.S. merchandise trade deficit announcement and the trade restriction and conflict events contain some new information about the profit future of the trade related firms, they should be immediately reflected in these firms' stock prices.

The purpose of this study is to investigate the possible effects of trade related news on the stock price movements of the U.S. import-competing and Korean and Taiwanese export-oriented firms. Although several studies have investigated the impact of trade deficit news and trade restrictions on stock prices, they only focused on the U.S. market. Also the previous examinations of the trade deficit news effect on stock prices are only limited to the stock market indices. This study distinguishes from the existing trade news literature in three aspects. First, by extending the trade related news study to foreign markets, specifically to Taiwan and South Korea stock markets, this study tests the hypothesis that the U.S. trade protection and trade deficit news may affect some foreign markets more than they do the U.S. market. This hypothesis is based on trade theory that a small open economy (SOE) gains more from free trade than a large open economy (LOE). However, at the bargaining table the LOE has more bargaining power than the SOE because a LOE's market is much more valuable to the SOE than is the opposite. No doubt the U.S. economy is a LOE. Both Taiwan and South Korea are SOEs relative to the U.S. economy and their fast development heavily relied on exports. The U.S. market was particularly important to them. As indicated in Table 1.2, Taiwan and South Korea incurred a large trade surplus with the U.S. during the 1980s, especially when the surplus is measured as a percentage of their corresponding GNP. For Korea, the trade surplus with the U.S. as a percentage of GNP was above 7% in 1987 and 1988. For Taiwan, it has been above 10% since 1983 and reached a maximum of 19.15% in 1985. Compare these numbers with the trade deficit as a percentage of GNP in the U.S. during the same period (see Table 1.1), we find the percentage for the U.S. is much smaller. The highest for the U.S. occurred in 1987 which was 3.36%. In fact, during the 1980s, the U.S. often used its market power to challenge the so-called "unfair" traders, and Korea and Taiwan were frequently named as unfair traders. Therefore it is very possible when the U.S. coughs, Korea and Taiwan sneeze. Korean and Taiwanese markets may be more sensitive to the U.S. trade related news than the U.S. market itself. The availability of the PACAP database[6] makes it possible to empirically test this hypothesis. The exploration of U.S. trade restriction and deficit effects on stock prices of Korean and Taiwanese firms is a novel aspect of this study.

Second, by examining the stock price response to trade deficit news on U.S. import-competing and Korean and Taiwanese export-oriented firms in addition to the market indices, this study tries to distinguish between the possible signals conveyed by the trade deficit news, and also reduce the watering down effect resulting from focusing on market indices. Previous authors have advanced several possible signals conveyed by the trade deficit news which might affect the stock market.[7] However, it is hard to distinguish the signals by examining the market indices only. As pointed out by Shapiro (1988), to a dynamic economy, a trade deficit is neither good nor bad. The stock market indices are proxies of the whole economy, thus, the signals conveyed by the trade deficit news are hard to read from the response of stock market indices. By examining trade related firms' stock price response, we can clear up some of the ambiguities. It is also reasonable to assume that the trade deficit news will have a more direct impact on U.S. import-competing firms and foreign export-oriented firms than on the market indices. Since the market indices include firms that are not closely related to foreign trade, trade deficit news effect on the indices may be "watered down" by these firms, especially if trade deficit news increases the probability of increasing

U.S. protection, or if it signals the further deteriorating competitiveness of U.S. import-competing firms.

Table 1.2

Korean and Taiwanese Bilateral Trade Surplus with the U.S. and the Surplus as a Percentage of Their GNP ($ in Billion)

Korea	Surplus	GNP	Surplus/GNP
1980	-0.43	55.57	-0.79%
1981	0.11	64.42	0.17%
1982	0.11	67.74	0.16%
1983	1.22	74.15	1.65%
1984	3.37	80.26	4.20%
1985	4.05	81.84	4.95%
1986	6.67	94.49	7.06%
1987	8.89	123.10	7.23%
1988	8.90	172.57	5.15%
Taiwan			
1980	2.25	40.77	6.25%
1981	3.76	45.98	8.18%
1982	4.51	46.66	9.66%
1983	6.53	51.51	12.68%
1984	9.77	61.10	15.99%
1985	11.70	61.09	19.15%
1986	14.27	79.29	17.99%
1987	17.21	111.02	15.50%
1988	12.67	126.05	10.05%

Sources: Computed from *U.S. Foreign Trade Highlights* (1988) and *International Financial Statistics Yearbook* (1986, 1992), United Nation.

Third, by using Korean and Taiwanese data, this study puts more emphasis on testing the hypotheses that the trade deficit news signals an increasing probability of raising protection in the foreseeable future (protection hypothesis) and its competing hypothesis that the trade deficit news signals the further deteriorating competitiveness of U.S. import-competing firms (competitiveness hypothesis). These two hypotheses seem to be more related to the strong protection sentiment existing in the U.S. It is reasonable to argue that the trade deficit news may have an impact on foreign exchange markets and the consequent exchange rate changes may have a direct impact on trade related firms' stock prices. Therefore, the trade deficit news effect on trade related firms' stock prices is complicated by its simultaneous impact on exchange rates. However, for most of the 1980s, both the Korean won and new Taiwanese dollar were pegged to the U.S. dollar. This greatly reduces the possibility that the trade deficit news had an impact on Korean and Taiwanese export-oriented firms' stock prices via exchange rate changes, and thus allows us to focus on testing other hypotheses such as the protection hypothesis and the competitiveness hypothesis.

In this study the trade related news is divided into two types—the regularly announced news such as the monthly U.S. merchandise trade deficit announcements and the nonregularly announced news such as U.S. trade restrictions against Taiwan and South Korea, and U.S-Taiwan, U.S-Korea trade conflict events. The nonregular news can be further divided into general events and specific events. The general events are concerned with the general trade relationship between the U.S. and Taiwan or Korea and consequently would have a general impact on all export-oriented firms in Taiwan or Korea. The specific events refer to the trade restrictions or trade conflicts which would mainly affect the export-oriented firms of Taiwan or Korea in a specific industry. Hopefully by focusing on the trade related firms and extending to foreign markets, this study can shed some light on the information content implicit in the trade related news. The previous studies on U.S. trade deficit news, trade restrictions and their impact on asset pricing are reviewed in Chapter 2. Chapter 3 provides a general analytical framework and describes the empirical models that will be used in the later chapters. Chapters 4 through 6 examine the possible effect of trade related news on the U.S. import-competing firms and Korean and Taiwanese export-oriented firms respectively. Chapter 7 compares the empirical results across countries and concludes the paper.

Notes

---

[1] See "Message from the chairman," *USITC Annual Report 1980.*

[2] See "Message from the chairman" in *USITC Annual Report 1982.*

[3] Escape clause cases are regulated by section 201 of the Trade Act of 1974. According to Pearson (1989), they "give perhaps the clearest evidence of executive tilt for or against protection." (See Chapter Two of his book).

[4] Section 301 of 1974 Trade Act.

[5] For a survey of many of these studies and models see Hartigan (1981).

[6] Pacific-Basin Capital Market Database compiled by The University of Rhode Island.

[7] See Chapter 2 of this study for a more detailed review.

II

Literature Review

It is well known that in an efficient market, asset prices have incorporated all the available information so that the price movement is solely caused by newly arrived information. If trade restriction events and the monthly U.S. merchandise trade deficit announcement contain some information which has not been anticipated by the market, they should shift the relevant asset prices, such as stock prices and foreign exchange rates.

Based on the above logic, several authors have examined the financial market response to U.S. trade deficit announcements and trade restriction events. They are going to be reviewed along three strands in this Chapter: a) Trade restrictions and their impact on the stock prices of U.S. import-competing firms; b) Trade deficit announcements and stock indices; and c) trade deficit announcements and foreign exchange rates. In addition, a brief review will be given for the studies which analyse the relationship between stock prices and foreign exchange rate changes. Since it is reasonable to assert that the exchange rate change will have a direct impact on the profitability of trade related firms and their stock prices, the trade deficit news effect on those firms' stock prices may be complicated by its simultaneous impact on exchange rates.

2.1 Trade Restrictions and U.S. Import-Competing Firms' Stock Prices

Hartigan, Perry and Kamma (1986) investigated trade restriction effects on the protection seeking firms' stock prices. The authors pointed out that international economists were often concerned with the impact of commercial policy on the level and distribution of national income, the structure of production and employment, and the level of imports. However, these studies did not provide detailed information on the more frequent government intervention in foreign trade at the firm or disaggregated industry level.

The authors focused their investigation on the protection decision effects of the escape clause (Section 201) petitions filed under the Trade Act of 1974 with the ITC. The U.S. government interventions often take place under the authority of the ITC, which handles petitions by business and labor requesting relief from the competitive pressures of imports or complaints about foreign unfair trade practices, etc.. The ITC conducts investigations and makes affirmative or negative rulings on these petitions. In some cases such as escape clause petitions, the ITC has to submit each affirmative ruling to the President as a policy recommendation. The President can accept, reject, or modify this recommendation.

Section 201 of the 1974 Trade Act provides a procedure whereby domestic industries seriously injured by increased imports can petition for import relief generally in the form of tariffs or quantitative restrictions. It is not necessary to prove that an unfair trade practice exists since the qualification for relief is that imports cause serious injury to the industry. Section 201 is based on article XIX of the General Agreement on Tariffs and Trade (GATT) which permits a country to "escape" temporarily from its free trade obligations under GATT. Therefore, Section 201 is also called the "escape clause". According to Finger et al (1982), Section 201 cases constitute the "high track" of Protection.

The authors identified 19 industries involved in Section 201 petitions and examined the USITC and presidential decision effects on these industries. First, a time series regression analysis was conducted by employing the market model from the standard capital market event study[1]. They examined the weekly cumulative abnormal return from two weeks before the petition date to four weeks after the final decision, the abnormal return of the ITC decision week, and the abnormal return of the presidential decision week. Surprisingly, the results were generally insignificant, i.e., the petition industries' stock returns did not respond to the administered protection. Then they went on to conduct a cross sectional regression which took into consideration the import penetration level and profitability of the firms in these industries. In this way they found significant results for protection decisions. An affirmative ITC ruling or presidential decision would have a positive impact on the industries' stock returns and a negative ITC decision would have a negative impact.

The authors interpreted their results by pointing out that first, cross sectional analysis was more powerful than time series analysis because cross sectional analysis introduces profitability and the degree of importance of the pertinent products to firm operations, while time series analysis treated all firms in an industry as if they were homogeneous; and second, the protection the firms in these industries sought from Section 201 were inherently temporary, so that the net benefit resulted from granting protection was small and the standard event study could not detect. They concluded that the benefits derived from protection by the petitioned industries were small and conditional on internal variables for each firm in these industries.

In another study, Hartigan, Kamma and Perry (1989) investigated the impact of nonsteel antidumping petitions filed under Section 731 on stock prices of the related firms. Under the Trade Reform Act of 1979, the structure of an antidumping investigation is as follows. When the firms file a petition, the ITC is responsible to make a preliminary injury determination. The criteria used for making an affirmative decision are injury to the pertinent firms, the threat of injury to these firms, and a combination of injury and threat of injury. If the ITC rulings are affirmative, the Department of Commerce (DOC) must start its investigation on whether there is dumping. If the final decision of the DOC is affirmative, then the ITC will make its final decision. If any of the above mentioned rulings are negative, the investigation terminates automatically. If the investigation gets through an affirmative ITC final decision, the U.S. Customs Service is instructed to apply an antidumping duty to the exports of the "guilty" firms.

The authors identified 47 such petitions with a total of 130 firms. Using weekly data and event study methodology, they found the USITC and the Department of Commerce rulings on these petitions did have an impact on the sample firms stock prices. More specifically, they found that "relief is valuable to these firms only when the USITC has determined that they are threatened with injury from imports priced below fair value. When there is evidence of actual injury, relief from dumping is not valuable."

Lenway, Reihbein and Starks (1990) examined the existence of wealth gains upon changes in trade protection for the U.S. steel industry. They argued that trade restrictions resulted in a wealth redistribution of income from consumers to the protected firms and the gain upon changes in protection for these firms should be reflected in their stock prices immediately. The authors identified six events which involved changes in trade protection for the steel industry from 1969 to 1982 and 22 firms in the industry. Using daily data and two modified versions of the market model[2], a portfolio approach and an unconstrained approach, they tested the impact of the six events on these firms and found some evidence in their results that an increase in protection level was associated with a positive abnormal return of the steel firms. They also found that the gains were unequally distributed among the firms depending on the size, market share, and profitability of the firms. The authors concluded that the increase in protection level did create statistically significant rents for the steel industry.

In view of the fact that about one-third of antidumping cases were withdrawn or voluntarily terminated, Prusa (1992) presented a bargaining model of the settlement process. His analysis showed that the antidumping petition can be used as a vehicle to achieve collusive outcomes. This is consistent with the data that the withdrawn cases had at least as great an effect on trade as cases with positive final ITC rulings.

2.2 Trade Deficit News and Stock Indices

Hardouvelis (1987) was the first to examine the stock price response to U.S. merchandise trade deficit announcements. In his study of stock price response to macroeconomic news, he regressed four U.S. stock index returns separately on 15 macroeconomic news variables including trade deficit news from 1979 to 1984. The trade deficit news was proxied by the deviation between the announced trade deficit and the expected trade deficit as a percentage of the expected trade deficit. For the whole period, the S&P 500 stock index return had no response to the trade deficit news. For the period 1979-1982 the response of the AMEX-MM index return to the trade deficit news was marginally significant, but for 1982-1984 the response was again insignificant. For 1979-1982 a surprisingly large

U.S. trade deficit was associated with an increase in the AMEX-MM index return. Hardouvelis did not identify the channels through which the trade deficit might operate on the stock indices. He thought the positive response of AMEX-MM was counter intuitive and might be caused by a short term interest rate change.

A more interesting study of the trade deficit news and its impact on the international financial market was provided by Puffer (1990). Puffer examined the trade deficit news effect on the Dow Jones Industrial Average (DJIA), Nikkei and Topix indices, the yen/dollar exchange rate, and the U.S. and foreign short term interest rates from 1980 to 1989. Her results showed that the overnight (close$_{t-1}$ to open$_t$) DJIA index return had a statistically significant negative response to the trade deficit announcement which came before the opening of the NYSE. A surprisingly large trade deficit was associated with a decrease in the DJIA index return. However, this response was not seen in either the following trading time (open$_t$ to close$_t$) return or the daily (close$_{t-1}$ to close$_t$) return around the trade deficit announcement. The reactions of Nikkei and Topix, and the short term interest rates on U.S. T-bill and the Eurocurrency deposits were all insignificant but the yen/dollar exchange rate did have a statistically significant response to the trade deficit news. A larger than expected trade deficit was associated with a depreciation of the dollar both overnight and during the trading time.

Puffer identified several possible channels through which the trade deficit news might affect stock price indices. First, the trade deficit is the major component of the current account. From the accounting identity the following must hold:

Current Account = Private - Private - Government Budget (2.1)
   Balance   Savings Investment   Deficit

Current Account = Domestic - Domestic = Net Foreign (2.2)
   Balance   Savings   Investment   Investment

Therefore, the trade deficit news may provide information about the international investment pattern, private and government spending and savings. Puffer went on to quote Shapiro (1989) " If the current-account deficit and the resulting capital account surplus finances productive investment, then the nation is better off; the returns from these added investments will service the foreign debts

and leave something extra. Conversely, a capital account surplus that
finances consumption will increase the nation's well-being today at
the expense of its future well-being."

Second, the trade deficit news may change market participants'
anticipation of future government policy responses. There are three
possible policy responses: currency devaluation, stabilization of
nominal dollar value, and increasing protection. Currency
depreciation is often used to combat an unexpectedly large trade
deficit. Government may devalue its currency by increasing money
supply. This may lead to dollar depreciation via two routes.
According to the traditional Keynesian model, increasing money
supply produces a liquidity effect which results in lower interest rates
and consequently higher stock index prices. However, an anticipated
increase in the money supply can also lead to inflation expectations
which will result in higher nominal interest rates, and consequently
lower stock index prices. The unexpectedly large trade deficit puts
downward pressure on the dollar value and Government may try to
defend or stabilize the dollar value. This can be done through a
contractional monetary policy which may also decrease or increase
the stock index prices depending on inflation expectations.
Increasing protection is a very possible response to large trade
deficits. However, protection will reduce domestic industries'
competitiveness in the long run, and thus have a negative impact on
stock indices.

Puffer's results were not consistent with the first channel, i.e.,
the trade deficit news effect on stock indices through the accounting
identity. For the second channel, her results were only consistent
with the policy response of protection. Puffer concluded that the New
York stock market responded to the U.S. trade deficit news but not
the Tokyo stock market. Also the response in the New York market
only showed in the overnight DJIA index return.

2.3 Trade Deficit News and Exchange Rates

Hardouvelis (1988) also examined the post-October 1979
response of exchange rates and interest rates to the new information
contained in the first announcement of 15 U.S. macroeconomic
series—including the trade deficit announcement series. He
hypothesized that a surprisingly large trade deficit would cause dollar

depreciation due to agents viewing such news as a signal of higher future trade deficits which would increase foreign holdings of U.S. dollar denominated assets. However, he found that a surprisingly large trade deficit had no statistically significant effect on the value of the dollar in the period 1979-1984.

Deravi, Gregorowicz and Hegji (1988) focused their attention on the effect of trade deficit announcements on exchange movements. They argued that if the Federal Reserve System had a trade balance target, then surprisingly large trade deficits would be likely to trigger foreign exchange market intervention aimed at dollar depreciation to reduce the trade deficit. Therefore, a surprisingly large trade deficit should be associated with dollar depreciation. Using the data of five bilateral dollar exchange rates for six major currencies covering the period February 1980-July 1987, they found little evidence of a response in foreign exchange markets to monthly trade deficit announcements prior to 1985. However, they found strong evidence during the post-1985 period that a dollar depreciation both in the spot and forward markets was associated with surprisingly large trade deficits.

Hogan, Melvin and Roberts (1990) also studied the trade deficit news effect on exchange rates. In addition to the channels mentioned by Hardouvelis and Deravi, Gregorowicz and Hegji above, the authors further hypothesized that the trade deficit news might operate on exchange rates through revisions of the probability of increased protectionist policies. However, this effect on exchange rates would be ambiguous. A smaller expected future trade deficit resulting from increased protection may be expected to lead to dollar appreciation. On the other hand, it is also possible that an increase in import restrictions may be associated with a higher expected U.S. price level which would in turn lead to dollar depreciation. Using dollar/pound, dollar/yen, and dollar/mark data from February 1980 to March 1989, the authors found that the trade deficit news had no statistically significant impact on the exchange rates for the entire period. Dividing the sample into two subperiods, February 1980 - April 1984 and May 1984 - March 1989, they found the trade deficit news effect in the second subperiod but not in the first one. In the second subperiod a surprisingly large trade deficit was associated with a depreciation of the dollar. This finding is consistent with the previous findings by Hardouvelis and Deravi, Gregorowicz and Hegji, i.e., in the first half of 1980s the trade deficit news had no impact on the exchange rates but in the second half it had. In view of this, the authors made another hypothesis that the trade deficit news effect on exchange rates were time-varying. Assuming a linear relationship between the news coefficient and the trade deficit level, the authors found some support for their hypothesis. In conjunction with their investigation on the trade deficit effects on interest rates, the authors claimed that the channels mentioned by Hardouvelis and Deravi, Gregorowicz and Hegji were less supported than the protection channel.

2.4 Exchange Rates and Stock Prices

Many authors have studied the relationship between stock prices and exchange rates. Among them are Frank and Young (1972), Ang and Ghallab (1976), Aggarwal (1981), Solnik (1987), and more recently, Soenen and Hennigar (1988). Basically the results showed that the exchange rate change and the stock price movement were correlated.

Soenen and Hennigar regressed the New York Stock Exchange Index, the S&P 500 Stock Index, and seven trade related industry's stock indices separately against a broad measure of the value of the U.S. dollar, the effective exchange rate of the U.S. dollar weighed against 15 other major currencies for the period of 1980-1986. They found that a) there was a strong negative relationship between the dollar value and the market indices, i.e., a depreciation of the dollar was associated with an increase in stock prices; b) the J-curve effect was not statistically significant, which is consistent with an efficient market; c) the responses of seven trade related industries' stock indices generally confirmed the negative relationship between security prices and exchange rates. Therefore, the hypothesis that a decline in the value of the home-currency is expected to stimulate trade related industries and the domestic economy as a whole can not be rejected.

2.5 Summary and Comments

The effect of protection events on the import-competing firms' stock prices are mixed. The decision effect of Section 201 cases can not be observed for petition firms as a whole in the market, however, the decision effect of Section 731 on petition firms has been observed. The effect of increased protection for the steel industry is also captured by steel firms. The study concerning Section 201 and Section 731 cases used weekly data and the study of the steel industry used daily data. Weekly data may contain more noise and, thus, weaken the effect.

The evidence of trade deficit news on stock indices are also mixed. Nikkei, Topix, and S&P 500 had no response to the trade deficit news, but the overnight return of the DJIA index had a positive response. This pattern suggests two possible explanations. First, the news effect might be contaminated by the noise contained in the daily data. The trade deficit news effect was only captured by the DJIA Index overnight return but not by the return of the trading time that followed and the daily return which includes both periods. However, the fact that the overnight index return in the Tokyo market did not show any response, weakens this explanation. Second, the news effect might be watered down by non-trade related firms included in the Nikkei, Topix, and S&P 500. All these indices include more than 400 firms, while the DJIA index only includes 30 blue chip firms which may be reasonably assumed to have more international exposure than other firms.

Puffer identified several channels through which the trade deficit news may operate on stock prices. However, the linkages are not very obvious and the translation processes are complicated by interest rates, inflation expectations, exchange rates, etc.. If attention is paid on trade related firms, then the signal should be more clear and the linkages more direct. Also, by focusing on trade related firms, the "watering down" effect of using stock indices can be reduced.

The important information content implicit in the trade deficit news appears that it signals a possible shift of the protection level in the future. Although Puffer identified several ways the trade deficit news might operate on stock prices, she claimed that her result was only consistent with the protection hypothesis. Hogan, Melvin, and Roberts's evidence also suggests that the trade deficit news effect on exchange rates more likely operates through the changing expectation of the future protection level than through the other channels.

Built on the above authors' analyses, this study will investigate the stock price responses of U.S. import-competing firms and Korean and Taiwanese export-oriented firms to the trade protection events and the trade deficit news.

Notes

---

[1] See Chapter 3 (section 3.3) for detail.
[2] See Chapter 3 (section 3.3) for detail.

III

Trade News and Stock Prices

3.1 A Dynamic Setup

In the simple efficient markets model, the stock price P_t of a share at the beginning of the time period t is given by

$$P_t = \sum_{k=0}^{\infty} \frac{E_t D_{t+k}}{(1+r)^{k+1}} \tag{3.1}$$

where D_t is the dividend paid at the end of time t, E_t denotes the mathematical expectation conditional on information available at time t, and r is the expected cost of equity or required rate of return on equity for k+1 periods, i.e.,

$$r = E_t \{(1+r_t)(1+r_{t+1})...(1+r_{t+k})\}^{1/(k+1)} - 1 \tag{3.2}$$

r_{t+k} for k≥0 is determined by the security market line,

$$r_{t+k} = R_{f,t+k} + b_{t+k}(R_{m,t+k} - R_{f,t+k}) \tag{3.3}$$

where R_f and R_m are the risk free rate and the market rate respectively, and ß is the systematic risk of the firm. Therefore, r depends on the current and the expected future path of R_f, R_m and ß.

Following Shiller (1981), we adopt the innovation notation which will facilitate our analysis. We define the innovation operator as $\sigma_t \equiv E_t - E_{t-1}$. Then for any variable X_t, we can write

$$\sigma_t X_{t+k} = E_t X_{t+k} - E_{t-1} X_{t+k} \tag{3.4}$$

namely, $\sigma_t X_{t+k}$ represents the change in the conditional expectation of X_{t+k} that is made in response to newly arrived information between time t-1 and t. Since conditional operators satisfy $E_j E_k = E_{min(j,k)}$,

$$E_{t-m}\sigma_t X_{t+k} = E_{t-m}(E_t X_{t+k} - E_{t-1} X_{t+k}) = E_{t-m} X_{t+k} - E_{t-m} X_{t+k} = 0 \tag{3.5}$$

where $m \geq 1$.

The implication from (3.5) is that $\sigma_t X_{t+k}$ must be uncorrelated with $\sigma_{t'} X_{t+j}$, $t' < t$ for all js and ks. This means that innovations in expectations are serially uncorrelated, which is consistent with efficient markets.

We know for one period holding, the stock price is:

$$P_t = \frac{D_t + E_t P_{t+1}}{1 + r_t} \tag{3.6}$$

or

$$E_t P_{t+1} = P_t (1 + r_t) - D_t \tag{3.7}$$

Therefore,

$$\sigma_t P_t \equiv E_t P_t - E_{t-1} P_t = P_t + D_{t-1} - P_{t-1}(1 + r_{t-1}) = \Delta P_t + D_{t-1} - P_{t-1} r_{t-1} \tag{3.8}$$

where $\Delta P_t = P_t - P_{t-1}$; $D_{t-1} - r_{t-1} P_{t-1}$ is the adjustment for the dividend paid out at the end of time t-1 and the time value of P_{t-1}. Both D_{t-1} and $r_{t-1} P_{t-1}$ are in the information set at time t and they constitute a forecastable part of the price innovation. However, $D_{t-1} - r_t P_{t-1}$ is negligible in the data set that we are going to use. Therefore, $\sigma_t P_t$ is approximately equal to the price change, ΔP_t. According to Samuelson (1965), $\sigma_t P_t$ is unforecastable by efficient markets.

On the basis of the above analysis, we have

$$\Delta P_t \cong \sigma_t P_t = \sigma_t \sum_{k=0}^{\infty} \frac{D_{t+k}}{(1+r)^{k+1}} = \sigma_t \left\{ \sum_{k=0}^{\infty} D_{t+k} \prod_{j=0}^{k} \frac{1}{1+r_{t+j}} \right\} \qquad (3.9)$$

This means that the price change depends on the innovation of the discounted future dividend stream. Any new information which can cause a revision of the expected future dividend stream and/or the discount rate will affect the stock price.

Suppose that the discounted future dividend stream is determined by a vector of fundamentals related to the earning power[1] and the discount rate, then the innovation of price will be affected by the innovations of all these fundamentals. For trade related firms, we can identify two fundamentals, trade restrictions TR and the exchange rates. For U.S. import-competing firms, an increase in the protection level, no matter if it is in the form of a tariff or non-tariff, will increase the barrier for foreign competitors. It will, in turn, increase the market power and profitability for the protected firms. The increased protection may also reduce the systematic risk ß for the protected firms because increased market power reduces the uncertainty these firms face relative to the market. For foreign export-oriented firms in general, if the protection is directed against them, they will lose their market share and their ß may also increase. *Ceteris paribus*, they should be made worse off. Therefore, an increase in U.S. trade protection will have a positive impact on the share prices of the protected firms and a negative impact on the share prices of the foreign rival firms.

Unexpected exchange rate changes may also have a significant impact on the share prices of trade related firms. A dollar depreciation will enhance the U.S. import-competing firms' competitiveness in the market because after a depreciation the dollar price of imported goods will increase and thus decrease the sales of foreign competitors; while a dollar appreciation will enhance foreign rival's competitiveness and hurt U.S. firms. Ceteris paribus, a dollar depreciation is expected to associate with a positive (negative) stock price movement of U.S. import-competing (foreign export-oriented) firms. However, this relationship may not hold when the depreciation is associated with a fostered inflation expectation.

3.2 *How Trade Related News Affects Stock Prices*

The innovation of the stock price of trade related firms can be expressed as a function of innovations of a set of fundamentals Zt plus the innovations of trade protection and the exchange rate,

$$\sigma_t P_t = f\left(\sigma_t \sum_{k=0}^{\infty} Z_{t+k} \quad \sigma_t \sum_{k=0}^{\infty} TR_{t+k} \quad \sigma_t \sum_{k=0}^{\infty} s_{t+k} \right) \qquad (3.10)$$

This indicates that a revision in the expectation of trade protection and/or a revision in expectation of the exchange rate will affect stock prices. It is reasonable to assume that the trade related news may cause revisions of expectations of these variables. Trade conflict and restriction events and trade deficit announcements are the two types of major trade news which have caused a great deal of public attention. In this section we discuss how trade news may affect trade related firms' stock prices.

3.2.1 *Trade Protection News and Stock Prices*

We define trade protection news as all the newly arriving trade conflict events, trade restriction events, and trade restriction seeking events. For example, a U.S. threat to retaliate against a country if it failed to meet the U.S. standard of "fair trade" is a trade conflict event; an affirmative decision made by the ITC on an "unfair trade" case is a trade restriction event; and a petition filed with the ITC by a U.S. firm seeking import relief is a restriction seeking event.

A trade restriction event actually shifts the current protection level, while a trade restriction seeking event or a trade conflict event may increase the probability of changing the protection level in the near future. Assuming such an event is unanticipated and arrives between time t-1 and t, it will be incorporated in E_t but not E_{t-1}. Thus, it will cause revision in the expectation of the protection path, i.e.,

$$\sigma_t \sum_{k=0}^{\infty} TR_{t+k} = E_t \sum_{k=0}^{\infty} TR_{t+k} - E_{t-1} \sum_{k=0}^{\infty} TR_{t+k} \neq 0 \qquad (3.11)$$

This revision, by equation (3.10), should be reflected in the stock price immediately. For U.S. import-competing firms as analyzed in the previous section, if the events increase the protection level or increase the probability of raising protection in the future, their stock prices will go up. For Asian export-oriented firms, if the protection events are directed against them, their stock price will move down. The reverse is true if the events reduce the protection level or reduce the probability of increasing protection level.

The protection news may also affect the expected path of exchange rates. First, some trade conflict news is directly related to the exchange rate. For example, in the mid-1980s, the U.S. pressured both Taiwan and Korea to appreciate their currencies against the dollar. These events might have affected both the expectation of protection and the expectation of exchange rate change because the uncertainty of whether Taiwan and Korea would agree to appreciate their currencies against the dollar might cause a revision of the expected exchange rate moving path, while at the same time Taiwan and Korea would face retaliation in the form of increasing trade restriction if they fail to appreciate their currencies. In either situation the event would have a positive impact on U.S. import-competing firms' stock prices and a negative impact on Asian export-oriented firms' stock prices. Second, if a protection event is so profound that the value of imports is greatly reduced, then the demand for foreign exchange will also decrease and the dollar value will increase. This dollar appreciation will work in the opposite direction to the increased protection level and offset some of its impact on the stock prices. However, this is only a side effect. In view of the U.S. trade protection events in the 1980s, this side effect should, at most, be small because the U.S. trade restriction had usually been product specific and temporary and therefore would not significantly affect the exchange rate.

On the whole, an increase in protection or an increase in the probability of increased protection is good news to U.S. import-competing firms and thus increases their stock prices, but bad news to Korean and Taiwanese export-oriented firms if the protection is directed against them, and thus decreases their stock prices.

3.2.2 Trade Deficit News and Stock Prices

Following previous authors, the trade deficit news is defined as the percentage forecast error of the monthly trade deficit, i.e., the monthly Commerce Department announced trade deficit minus the expected trade deficit, which is compiled by Money Market Services Inc. (MMS), divided by the expected trade deficit:

$$\text{Trade Deficit News} = (\text{Announced Deficit - Expected Deficit}) \div (\text{Expected Deficit}) \qquad (3.12)$$

In order to study the trade deficit effect on stock prices, it is necessary to identify what information content is implicit in the trade deficit news. A review of the causes of and the policies to combat trade deficits will shed some light on the possible information content.

The study of the causes of and the cures for the large trade deficit or current account deficit is, like the trade deficit itself, enormous. Although the causes of a trade deficit are in dispute, they can be classified into two groups: macroeconomic causes and microeconomic causes. Two major events occurred in the late 1970s and early 1980s that are commonly agreed as macro economic causes of the large U.S. trade deficit, 1) the rise in U.S. aggregate demand relative to foreign aggregate demand; and 2) the appreciation of the U.S. dollar which peaked in 1985. Macroeconomic theory indicates that imports are a positive function of aggregate demand and predicts that a rise in U.S. aggregate demand relative to foreign aggregate demand will increase U.S. imports more than U.S. exports to the rest of the world, thus resulting in a trade deficit. Also, an appreciation of the dollar will encourage U.S. imports and discourage U.S. exports, and thus lead to a U.S. trade deficit. In addition to the macroeconomic causes, many microeconomic factors have been advanced to explain the trade deficit. Among them: 1) noncompetitive wage demands by U.S. labor; 2) overly restrictive union-sponsored work rules; 3) subsidization of industries by foreign governments; 4) OPEC cartel activity; 5) inadequate R&D investment by U.S. firms; 6) distortional U.S. tax policy; and 7) overly restrictive antitrust policies.

Hilke and Nelson (1988) conducted an extensive study of all the above macro and micro causes. Their statistical analysis indicates that for the period 1975-1984, it was the macro instead of micro factors that caused the large U.S. trade deficit. Their results showed that there was no sudden fundamental change in all seven microeconomic factors mentioned above, so they could not be important causes of the deficit. On the other hand, their results did show that the rise in interest rates with the associated increase in the value of the dollar and, during some periods, the relatively rapid growth of U.S. aggregate demand, stimulated net imports.

At a January 1987 Brookings workshop on the U.S. current account imbalance, a set of uniform simulation results of 12 econometric models were compared (Bryant, Holtham, and Hooper ed. 1988). The consensus was that the deficit in the period 1980-1986 was caused mainly by two macroeconomic variables: the appreciation of the dollar and the relatively fast growth of the U.S. economy earlier in the decade. The persistence of the deficit after the dollar started to depreciate in 1985 was attributed to the time lag and inconsistent macro policies adopted by the leading industrial countries, e.g., the U.S. adopted a more expansionary fiscal policy than Japan and Germany while the opposite was needed.

Hooper and Mann (1989) examined the causes of emergence and persistence of the U.S. external deficit for the period of 1980-1987. By employing both partial equilibrium and general equilibrium approaches, their results showed that the two commonly agreed macro factors can explain about two-thirds, but not all, of the deficit, especially not the persistence of the deficit after the dollar depreciation of 1985. They further investigated the pricing strategies of U.S. and foreign firms and found that while U.S firms adjusted their product prices quickly in response to the exchange rate changes, foreign firms seemed to follow a strategy of pricing to the U.S. market, i.e., when the dollar appreciated the foreign firms raised their product price for their exports to the U.S. to make more profit and, when the dollar depreciated, these firms squeezed their profit margin by reducing the price of goods sold in the U.S. market. This pricing strategy together with other factors such as foreign protection and "unfair trade practices" contributed to the persistence of the trade deficit.

In short, these studies, like most of the other studies on this issue, suggest that the strong dollar and the fast growth of U.S. aggregate expenditure in the early 1980s were the major causes for building up the large trade deficit. However, the persistence of the trade deficit in the late 1980s can not be fully explained by these two causes. Some micro factors, such as the price to market strategy followed by foreign export-oriented firms and foreign protection may contribute to this persistence.

Three policy proposals were advanced by these authors: a) fiscal co-operation among the leading industrial countries, e.g., the surplus countries like Japan and Germany should expand their expenditures while the U.S. reduces its spending; b) further depreciating the dollar; and c) reducing trade restrictions both at home and abroad.

From the perceived causes of and suggested policy responses to the trade deficits, market participants may infer some signals from the trade deficit news. If market participants perceived that an unexpected larger U.S. trade deficit was caused by the two macroeconomic factors, they would anticipate the government to combat the deficit by 1) reducing government expenditure and 2) depreciating the dollar. Reducing government expenditure will have a general negative impact at home, not just on import-competing firms. Also, reducing government spending will reduce the government deficit and bring down interest rates and exchange rates if the strong dollar were caused by high interest rates, and thus have a secondary effect which is positive on import-competing firms. So the total effect on U.S. import-competing firms' stock price is ambiguous. However, reducing government spending would have a negative impact on Korean and Taiwanese export-oriented firms' stock prices because their exports depend heavily on the U.S. market.

Due to institutional reasons, fiscal policy is rather rigid, while intervening in the foreign exchange market is more flexible. Ceteris paribus, a devaluation of the dollar will benefit the import-competing firms but hurt foreign export-oriented firms, thus causing a positive stock price movement of the import-competing firms and a negative price movement of the foreign export-oriented firms. It is possible that a devaluation is associated with a higher inflation expectation which may more than offset the effect of the dollar devaluation. In such a situation, the impact on foreign export-oriented firms will not be negative, and the impact on U.S. import-competing firms will be negative. However, the higher inflation expectation will affect the whole economy. Therefore, we can tell whether an exchange rate depreciation is associated with a higher inflation expectation by comparing the stock price response of U.S. import-competing firms with the response of U.S. market indices. For most of the 1980s, the

Korean won and new Taiwanese dollar (NT$) were pegged to the U.S. Dollar so that a dollar depreciation would negatively affect their export-oriented firms' stock prices only when the depreciation actually changed won/US$ and NT$/US$ pegging rates.

Also the market participants may perceive that an unexpectedly larger U.S. trade deficit will increase the probability of imposition of future U.S. trade restrictions. This signal may not be read from the previous analyses of the causes and the cures of a trade deficit. Previous studies generally agreed that foreign "unfair trade practices" and other microeconomic factors were not the major causes underlying the large trade deficit although the price to market strategy of the foreign firms did explain, to a certain extent, the persistence of the trade deficit. Moreover, most researchers agreed that increasing protection would not be a good policy to reduce the trade deficit. However, the protectionist sentiments were strong. As mentioned before, even the Reagan administration had to bend to this pressure. This was because 1) although the micro factors were not the major cause for the trade deficit, some industries had been hurt by imports; 2) some powerful interest groups had taken the trade deficit and foreign "unfair trade practices" as excuses to seek rent from protection; 3) the government itself may be tempted to use protection as an alternative to combat the trade deficit, especially when it faces difficulties in cutting spending and in intervening in the foreign exchange market. Therefore, as long as the trade deficit news fuels the protectionist sentiment and the government may respond by increasing protection, the trade deficit news will signal to the market participants that the probability of imposing new trade restrictions is increased. If this is the case, then an unexpectedly large trade deficit will be associated with a positive movement of U.S. import-competing firms' stock prices and a negative movement of Korean and Taiwanese export-oriented firms' stock prices if the protection was aimed at them.

Another plausible possibility is that the trade deficit signals higher future trade deficits because of declining competitiveness of U.S. import-competing firms. Therefore, a surprisingly large trade deficit should be associated with a negative stock price movement of U.S. import-competing firms but a positive stock price movement of Korean and Taiwanese export-oriented firms. However, no matter whether the trade deficit news signals increasing protection or decreasing competitiveness, its expected impact on stock indices will be small because of the watering down effect.

Table 3.1

Hypothesized Trade Deficit News Signals and the Expected Signs of Their Impacts on Stock Prices

Stock Return Response	U.S. Import-Competing Firms	U.S. Market Return	Taiwanese & Korean Export-Oriented Firm
Reducing Gov't Spending	?	−	−
Dollar Depreciation without Inflation	+	?	−
Dollar Depreciation with Inflation	-	-	+
Increasing Protection	+	?	-
Losing Competitiveness	−	?	+

Note: + denotes positive impact; - negative; and ? ambiguous.

Table 3.1 summarizes the expected trade deficit news effect on stock prices of U.S. import-competing and Korean and Taiwanese export-oriented firms under five different hypothesized signals that the trade deficit news may convey. The trade deficit news can affect the stock prices via each of the five possible signals or all of these signals simultaneously. It is instructive to further distinguish among these signals and this will be done in the following chapters.

3.3 How to Measure the Trade News Effect

Three empirical models are employed in this study to test the trade news effect on U.S. import-competing and Korean and Taiwanese export-oriented firms' stock prices. For trade restriction and trade conflict events, we invoke 1) the capital market event study method—the market model; and 2) a modified version of the capital market event study—the seemingly unrelated regression (SUR) model. For trade deficit news, we follow Hardouvelis (1987), and employ a simple ordinary least square (OLS) regression model.

3.3.1 The Capital Market Event Study

The capital market event study was pioneered by Fama, Fisher, Jensen and Roll (1969). Since then, it has been widely used in the finance, accounting and economics literature. The capital market study method assesses the impact of a specific event on the value of a firm's common stock. In many cases, this method has also been used to measure the impact of government regulation and court decisions on individual firms. Schwert (1981) discussed this methodology in some detail. Brown and Warner (1980, 1985) conducted extensive simulation experiments and their results justified the use of this method.

We use this method to examine whether the appeal for protection and subsequent U.S. ITC decisions affect the U.S. protection-seeking firms' stock prices. If these protection-seeking events have no impact on the stock prices, then the protection-seeking firms will only earn normal returns which can be predicted by the well-known market model:

$$R_{it} = \alpha_i + \beta_i R_{mt} + \varepsilon_{it} \qquad (3.13)$$

where

    R_{it} = the rate of return for security i on day t;
    R_{mt} = the rate of return for the equally weighted CRSP market
            return on day t;
    α_i = a constant for security i;
    β_i = the systematic risk of security i;
    ε_{it} = disturbance term satisfying the classical conditions.

If the protection-seeking events do have an impact on the stock prices, then the protection-seeking firms will earn "abnormal returns" — returns significantly above or below that predicted by the market model. We designate the event day as day zero; day -10 to day 10 (10 days before the event to 10 days after the event) as the event period; and day -230 to day -11 as the estimation period. Using daily data in the estimation period we can estimate (3.13) for each security i in the portfolio of protection-seeking firms. Assuming that the estimated α_i, and β_i, are stable over the whole sample period, we can calculate the abnormal return AR_{it} for the days in the event period:

$$AR_{it} = R_{it} - E(R_{it}) = R_{it} - a_i - b_i R_{mt} \quad (t = -10, -9, ..., 9, 10) \quad (3.14)$$

where $E(R_{it})$ is the expected return based on market model. Then the average abnormal return (AAR) for each day in the event period and the average cumulative abnormal return (ACAR) for the event period can be calculated:

$$AAR_t = \sum_{i=1}^{n} \frac{AR_{it}}{n} \qquad t = (-10, -9, ..., 10) \qquad (3.15)$$

$$ACAR_t = \sum_{t=-10}^{T} AAR_t \qquad T = (-10, -9, ..., 10) \qquad (3.16)$$

where n denotes the number of securities in the portfolio.

The significance of the AAR and ACAR can be tested. However, more recent event studies do not test AARs and ACARs. Instead, ARs in the event period are standardized before they are aggregated, and the standardized aggregates form the basis of the test statistics. The approach, originally proposed by Patell (1976), was popularized in the finance literature by Dodd and Warner (1983). The SPE_{it}, the standardized prediction error for stock i at time t, is computed as follows:

$$SPE_{it} = \frac{AR_{it}}{s_{ft}} \qquad t = (-10, -9, ..., 10) \qquad (3.17)$$

The standardized error of forecast is defined as:

$$s_{ft} = s_i \sqrt{1 + (1/k) + \frac{(R_{mt} - R_m)^2}{\sum_{t=1}^{k} (R_{mt} - R_m)^2}} \qquad (3.18)$$

where k is the number of days in the estimation period (220 days in our case);

$$R_m = \frac{1}{k} \sum_{t=1}^{k} R_{mt} \qquad (3.19)$$

is the average market return in the estimation period;

$$s_i = \sqrt{\frac{\sum_{t=1}^{k} (\varepsilon_{it} - \mu_i)^2}{k}} \qquad (3.20)$$

is the standard error of the residuals in the estimation period and μ_i is the average residual.

With respect to equation (3.18), the 1/k term under the radical adjusts for the length of the estimation interval. The greater the k, the less error in the out of sample forecast, assuming stability in the relationship. The last term under the square root accounts for the induced error if R_{mt} varies significantly from what was observed in the estimation period. S_{ft} adjusts for any increase in variance during the event period which is not captured in the S_i.

The test statistic for a portfolio of n stocks on a particular day during the event period is

$$Z_{SPE} = \frac{\sum_{i=1}^{n} SPE_i}{\sqrt{n}} \qquad \sim N(0,1) \qquad (3.21)$$

The standardized cumulative prediction error for stock i is the sum of the SPE_i between any two days of interest in the event period, adjusted for the number of days $(t_2 - t_1 + 1)$ being considered:

$$SCPE_i = \frac{\sum_{t=t_1}^{t_2} SPE_{it}}{\sqrt{t_2 - t_1 + 1}} \qquad (3.22)$$

The test statistic for n stocks is the sum of the $SCPE_i$ divided by the square root of the number of stocks in the portfolio:

$$Z_{SCPE} = \frac{\sum_{i=1}^{n} SCPE_i}{\sqrt{n}} \qquad \sim N(0,1) \qquad (3.23)$$

There are two points worth mentioning when using daily data to estimate the market model. First, because of non-synchronous trading, the daily return may exhibit autocorrelation which leads to a biased estimation of ß. Scholes and Williams (1977) and Dimson (1979) have discussed this in detail and provided the modified estimation techniques which can correct the bias caused by the autocorrelation. Second, according to Brown and Warner (1985), the testing power of the market model is generally good except when there exists risk clustering and event day clustering simultaneously. Risk clustering refers to the firms under investigation being concentrated in the same industry; while event day clustering refers to all the events occurring on the same calendar date. If both types of clustering occur together, there will be a high degree of cross-sectional dependence and heteroscedasticity in the market model residuals thus rendering the calculated statistics unreliable. In such a case, the market model is not a good specification to capture the event effect.

In reality, the simultaneous occurrence of both clusterings are not rare. In this study, the trade restriction events related to Korean and Taiwanese export-oriented firms are industry specific, hence will affect all the firms in the same industry, which is exactly the simultaneous occurrence of both types of clustering. In addition, the non-synchronous trading problem is more severe for Korean and Taiwanese data. Therefore, we will turn to a modified version of the market model which can overcome these problems.

3.3.2 A Modified Version of the Market Model (SUR)

Shipper and Thomson (1983), Binder (1985 a, b, 1988), Rose (1985), Smith, Bradley and Jarrell (1986), Cornett and Tehranian (1989, 1990), and Lenway, Rehbein and Starks (1990) have applied the SUR model to their event studies. They used this model because it explicitly incorporates heteroskedasticity across equations and contemporaneous dependence of the disturbances into the hypothesis tests. In this model, the return generating process is conditioned on the occurrence and nonoccurrence of an event which is accomplished by appending a zero-one dummy variable to the market model equation. Following Cornett and Tehranian (1990),

$$R_{jt} = \alpha_j + \beta_{j1}R_{mt-2} + \beta_{j2}R_{mt-1} + \beta_{j3}R_{mt} + \beta_{j4}R_{mt+1} + \beta_{j5}R_{mt+2} + \sum_{k=1}^{k} \gamma_{jk}D_{kt} + \varepsilon_{jk}$$

$$j=1, 2, ..., J; \qquad t=1, 2, ..., T \qquad\qquad (3.24)$$

where

R_{jt} = the return on portfolio (or firm) j on day t;
R_{mt} = the return to the market proxy on day t;
α_j = an intercept coefficient for portfolio (or firm) j on day t;
β_{j1} to β_{j5} = risk coefficients for the jth portfolio (or firm);
γ_{jk} = the effect of event k on the jth portfolio (or firm);
D_{kt} = dummy variables which equal 1 during the period of the kth event and 0 otherwise; and
ε_{jt} = random disturbances which are assumed to satisfy the classical conditions.

The lags and leads of the market return in the model are used to adjust for non-synchronous trading.

We can also write the model in matrix form (see Theil 1971, p. 306):

$$
\begin{bmatrix} R_1 \\ R_2 \\ \cdots \\ R_j \end{bmatrix} = \begin{bmatrix} \overline{X} & 0 & \cdots & 0 \\ 0 & \overline{X} & \cdots & 0 \\ \cdots & \cdots & \cdots & \cdots \\ 0 & \cdots & \cdots & \overline{X} \end{bmatrix} \begin{bmatrix} \Gamma_1 \\ \Gamma_2 \\ \cdots \\ \Gamma_\varphi \end{bmatrix} + \begin{bmatrix} e_1 \\ e_2 \\ \cdots \\ e_j \end{bmatrix} \tag{3.25}
$$

where

$R_j = (R_{j1}, R_{j2}, ..., R_{jT})'$, a $T \times 1$ vector;
$\overline{X}$ = a $T \times (K+6)$ matrix of independent variables which is the
   same for each equation in the system;
Γ_j = a $(K+6) \times 1$ vector of coefficients;
e_j = a $T \times 1$ vector of disturbances.

More compactly,

$$
\mathbf{R = X\Gamma + E} \tag{3.26}
$$

   Within this system, the disturbance terms are assumed to be serially independent with a stationary cross-sectional covariance structure represented by the contemporaneous residual covariance matrix $\Sigma J \times J$. Thus, E has covariance matrix of $\Sigma \otimes I$. Since the explanatory variables are identical for each equation, OLS estimation provides identical parameter estimates to GLS. However, as pointed out by Shipper and Thomson, two hypotheses concerning the γ_{jk} can be tested within this framework. The first is that the sum (across the J portfolios or firms) of the event parameters for a particular trade protection event is equal to zero:

$$
H_0^1: \sum_{j=1}^{j} \gamma_{jk} = 0 \tag{3.27}
$$

where k denotes a particular event. The sum of parameters reflects a total, sample-wide influence of the event which is analogous to the sample-wide abnormal return computed in the market model event study.

   The second hypothesis is that, for a particular event k, each individual γ_{jk} parameter is equal to zero:

$$H_0^2 : \gamma_{jk} = 0 \quad \forall j \tag{3.28}$$

This can detect the return response of each portfolio or firm within the sample.

Both hypotheses can be tested by formulating constraints on the values of coefficients and calculating the F-statistic (see Theil 1971, p.314)

$$F_{(q,J(T-K))} = \frac{(a - A\hat{\Gamma})'\{A[X'(\Sigma^{-1} \otimes I)X]^{-1}A'\}(a - A\hat{\Gamma})}{(R - X\hat{\Gamma})'(\Sigma^{-1} \otimes I)(R - X\hat{\Gamma})} \times \frac{J \times T - J \times K}{q} \tag{3.29}$$

where $a - A\hat{\Gamma} = 0$ is the matrix form of the corresponding linear constraints, and q and J(T - K) are the degrees of freedom. Since Σ is unknown, it is replaced by the OLS residual covariance matrix in calculating the F-statistic.

We will use the SUR model to examine the impact of trade restriction and trade conflict events on the stock prices of Korean and Taiwanese export-oriented firms.

3.3.3 Simple Regression Model

Following Hardouvelis (1987), Deravi, Gregorowic and Hegji (1988), and Hogan, Melvin and Roberts (1990), we use a simple OLS regression model to examine the trade deficit news effect on the stock prices of both U.S. import-competing and Korean and Taiwanese export-oriented firms. Since the trade deficit is regularly announced, if using the market model, the estimation period of later announcements will overlap with the previous announcements. Of course, we can exclude the previous announcement dates in the estimation period, however the simple OLS can do the job more conveniently.

$$R_{jt} = \alpha + \beta * NEWS_t + \varepsilon_{it} \tag{3.30}$$

where

R_{it} = the ith portfolio's return on day t,
$NEWS_t$ = the trade deficit news on day t,
α = an intercept term,
ß = news effect coefficient, and
$_{it}$ = residual term on day t for the ith portfolio or firm.

If the trade deficit news has an impact on the stock return, then ß should be significantly different from zero. Since the news effect may be time-varying with the trade deficit level, we follow Hogan, Melvin and Roberts (1990), to further hypothesize a linear relationship between the news coefficient and the trade deficit level,

$$\beta_t = c + d*DEF_t \qquad (3.31)$$

where DEF_t is the trade deficit level on day t; d is the coefficient of the deficit level. Substitute (3.31) into (3.30) and rearrange:

$$R_{jt} = a + c*NEWS_t + d*NEWS_t*DEF_t + e_{it} \qquad (3.32)$$

If d is significantly different from zero, then β_t is linearly varying with the deficit level. The time-varying news effect may be inferred from taking the partial derivative of (3.32) with respective to $NEWS_t$,

$$\frac{\partial R_{it}}{\partial NEWS_t} = c + dDEF_t = \beta_t \qquad (3.33)$$

We may test the average effect of β_t by substituting the mean of the trade deficit for DEF_t and calculate the t-statistic.

3.4 Summary

The theoretical relationships between various trade news and the stock prices of domestic and foreign trade related firms are discussed. It is hypothesized that, in general, the trade conflict and/or trade restriction news will have a positive impact on U.S. import-competing firms and a negative impact on Korean and Taiwanese export-oriented firms. The trade deficit news may convey five different signals each with its own implications on the U.S. market index, U.S. import-competing firms, and Korean and Taiwanese export-oriented firms. Three empirical models are described. The conventional market model will be used to test the impact of trade restriction news on U.S. import-competing firms. The modified version of market model (SUR) will be used to test the impact of trade conflict news on Korean and Taiwanese firms. The simple OLS model will be used to test the trade deficit effect on both U.S. import-competing and Korean and Taiwanese export-oriented firms.

Notes

[1] Earning are good indicators of future dividends.

IV

Empirical Investigation for U.S. Import-Competing Firms

4.1 Unfair Trade Practice Petitions and the Petitioners' Stock Prices

Previous authors have investigated the effect of escape clause petitions filed under the Trade Act of 1974 (section 201), the antidumping petitions filed under the Trade Reform Act of 1979 (section 731) on petition firms' stock prices and the effect of protection events on some specific industries such as the steel industry. In this section, we investigate the effect of the unfair trade practice petitions filed under the Tariff Act of 1930 (section 337).

"Section 337 declares unlawful unfair methods of competition and unfair acts in importation or sale of products in the United States, the threat or effect of which is to destroy or substantially injure a domestic industry, prevent the establishment of such an industry, or restrain or monopolize trade and commerce in the United States. Section 337 also declares as unlawful per se infringement of a valid and enforceable U.S. patent, copyright, registered trade mark, or mask work; no resulting injury need be found."[1]

After receipt of a petition, the ITC conducts investigations to determine whether unfair methods of competition or unfair acts are occurring in the importation of articles into the U.S. or in their sales. The investigation must be completed at most within 18 months after the date of publication of notice of investigation in the Federal Register. If the ITC finds the existence of unfair trade practices, it may issue orders excluding the articles from entry or issue cease and desist orders. The President may disapprove these actions within 60 days after issuance of the Commission's determination.

4.1.1 Data and Methodology

During the period 1980-1993, the ITC completed 314 investigations of cases involving unfair trade practice. Among them, 58 cases were identified from the USITC Annual Report with petition firms' daily stock return data available on the CRSP data tape around the petition day, the day when the petition appeared in the Federal Register. However, only 56 cases had data available around the final outcome day, i.e., the final ITC decision day or termination day (see Appendix A). In 16 out of the 58 cases, the final ITC ruling was in favor of the petitioners. In 29 cases, a settlement agreement was reached or the petition was voluntarily withdrawn, in 11 cases the final ITC decision was unfavorable to the petitioners.

Based on our discussion in chapter 3 (section 3.2.1), we hypothesize that the unfair trade practice petition increased the probability of increasing protection, and thus would have a positive impact on the petition firms' stock prices. The favorable outcome to these petitions actually increased the protection for petition firms, and thus would increase their stock prices; while an unfavorable outcome to these petitions would reverse the original expectation based on the petition, and thus would decrease the petition firms' stock prices. According to Prusa (1990), voluntarily terminated cases tend to involve collusion between the two parties, and, thus, would also increase the petitioners' stock prices.

In order to test the general effect of the unfair trade practice petitions and the subsequent outcomes, we invoke the capital market event study methodology as described in Chapter 3 (section 3.3.1). The market model (equation 3.13) is rewritten below:

$$R_{it} = \alpha_i + \beta_i R_{mt} + \varepsilon_i$$

This equation was estimated for each of the 58 firms in the portfolio by using daily returns from the estimation period (day -230 to -11 relative to the petition day). The estimated parameters[2] were then used to compute the abnormal returns for each day over the 21-day petition period (day -10 to day 10). Then, the average abnormal return (AAR), the average cumulative abnormal return (ACAR), the z-value of standardized prediction error (ZSPE) and the z-value of the standardized cumulative prediction error (ZSCPE) for the portfolio over the 21-day period were further computed. The same parameters were used to compute the same statistics for the 21-day outcome period (day -10 to day 10 relative to the final outcome day). Following our hypothesis, should the petition have a positive impact on the petition firms' stock prices, the ACAR over the petition period would be positive and the ZSCPE would be significantly different from zero. For the favorable and settlement outcomes, the ACAR and ZSCPE over the outcome period would be positive and significant; while for the unfavorable outcome, the ACAR and ZSCPE would be negative and significant.

4.1.2 Results

The results for the petition period is reported in Table 4.1. On day -3, the AAR for the portfolio of 58 petition firms is 0.6 percent and the ZSPE is 1.83 which is significant at the 10 percent level. On day 2, 4, and 9, the AARs are -0.4, -0.5, and -0.2 respectively. The corresponding ZSPEs are -2.46, -2.01, and -1.83, the first two are significant at the 5 percent level and the last one is significant at the 10 percent level. The positive AAR on day -3 may be consistent with the hypothesis that the petition creates positive abnormal returns for the protection seeking firms, but the negative AARs on day 2, 4 and 9 are not. The ACAR is plotted against the days in the petition period in Figure 4.1. From Figure 4.1 we see that the ACAR declines for the whole petition period. The 21-day cumulative abnormal return is -2.5 percent and the 21-day ZSCPE is -1.81, which is significant at the 10 percent level. This means that the petition would generate negative abnormal returns for the whole event period, which is inconsistent with our hypothesis. Considering the possibility that the event day might be the day when the petition was filed instead of the day when the petition was published in the Federal Register, the test was repeated for the window of 21-day period around the petition filing day. However, the results (not reported here) show no significant z-values throughout the event period, which is also inconsistent with our hypothesis.

Table 4.1

Test Statistics for the Portfolio of 58 U.S. Import-Competing Firms from 10 Days before to 10 Days after the Day (Day Zero) of the Petition Publication

DAY	AAR	ZSPE	ACAR	ZSCPE
-10	-0.00062326	-0.48291922	-0.00062326	-0.48291922
-9	-0.00106240	-0.02641393	-0.00168566	-0.36015292
-8	0.00373099	0.59744695	0.00204533	0.05087253
-7	-0.00367698	-0.40208501	-0.00163165	-0.15698560
-6	-0.00245261	-0.92651178	-0.00408426	-0.55476086
-5	-0.00047737	0.20671803	-0.00456163	-0.42203278
-4	-0.00424233	-0.75491013	-0.00880395	-0.67605564
-3	0.00583462	1.8274779*	-0.00296934	0.01371887
-2	-0.00447474	-0.76679126	-0.00744408	-0.24266281
-1	-0.00242035	-0.73921796	-0.00986443	-0.46397140
0	-0.00162305	-0.29324343	-0.01148748	-0.53079559
1	0.00337138	0.92605465	-0.00811611	-0.24086914
2	-0.00420636	-2.463458**	-0.01232247	-0.91466006
3	-0.00244924	-0.68312200	-0.01477171	-1.06396052
4	-0.00539441	-2.009293**	-0.02016612	-1.54668073
5	0.00571598	1.25105490	-0.01445014	-1.18480345
6	-0.00393177	-1.08330490	-0.01838192	-1.41216822
7	-0.00035234	0.02484748	-0.01873426	-1.36652421
8	-0.00412690	-1.10028447	-0.02286116	-1.58249957
9	-0.00186985	-1.8341691*	-0.02473101	-1.9525624*
10	-0.00047967	0.41936582	-0.02521068	-1.8139927*

Note: ** (*) denotes significance at the 5 (10) percent level.

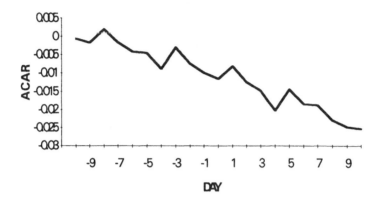

Figure 4.1 The ACAR for All Petition Firms during the Petition Period

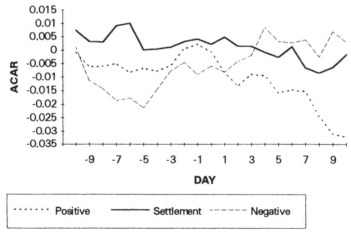

Figure 4.2 The ACAR for the Firms with Affirmative, Negative Final USITC Rulings and with Settlement Agreement during the Outcome Period

In order to examine the outcome effects on the petition firms, we further divide our sample into three groups based on whether the ITC decision is favorable to the petition firms, not favorable to the petition firms, or the cases were voluntarily terminated. Table 4.2 reports the results for the group of 16 cases with affirmative ITC decisions during the outcome period; Table 4.3 reports the results for the group of 29 cases with voluntary termination; and Table 4.4 reports the results for the group of 11 cases with negative ITC decisions. Their ACARs are plotted against the days during the outcome period in Figure 4.2. The results in Table 4.2 are counter-intuitive. We expect to find some positive and significant ZSPE around day zero because the affirmative ITC rulings would lead to increased protection for the petition firms. However, we only found negatively significant SZPEs on day 8 and day 9. On day 8, the AAR is -0.9 percent and the ZSPE is -2.92, which is significant at 5 percent. On day 9, the AAR is -0.68 percent and the ZSPE is -1.69 which is significant at 10 percent. In addition, the ACAR (see Figure 4.2) for the whole outcome period is -3.2 percent and the corresponding ZSCPE is -1.95, which is significant at 10 percent. This suggests that the affirmative ITC rulings bring negative rather than positive abnormal returns to the protection-seeking firms.

The results in Table 4.3 are also hard to explain. On day -10 the AAR is 0.75 percent and the ZSPE is 2.10, which is significant at 5 percent. On day -5 and day 7, the AARs are -1 percent and -0.8 percent respectively and the corresponding ZSPEs are -2.09 and -2.4, both significant at 5 percent. On day 10, the AAR is 0.5 percent and the ZSPE is 1.64, which is significant at the 10 percent level. This pattern is neither consistent with the collusion hypothesis advanced by Prusa nor consistent with the alternative hypotheses that the settlement agreements or voluntary termination of the cases should have no impact or negative impact on the petition firms. However, the ACAR seems not significantly different from zero (see Figure 4.2) and the ZSCPEs are not significant throughout the outcome period.

The results in Table 4.4 lend some weak support for the hypothesis that negative ITC rulings hurt petition firms. On day -9, the AAR is -1.2 percent and the ZSPE is -2.03, which is significant at t5 percent. The ACAR is negative from day -9 until day 3. The ZSCPE is significant from day -9 until day -5. The ACAR from day -10 to day -5 is -2.1 percent and the ZSCPE for the same period is

Table 4.2

Test Statistics for the Portfolio of 16 U.S. Import-Competing Firms from 10 Days before to 10 Days after the Day (Day Zero) of the Final USITC Affirmative Ruling

Day	AAR	ZSPE	ACAR	ZSCPE
-10	-0.00065724	-0.06307873	-0.00065724	-0.06307873
-9	-0.00546303	-0.48854905	-0.00612027	-0.39005974
-8	0.00011504	0.44903568	-0.00600523	-0.05923158
-7	0.00108383	-0.36354677	-0.00492140	-0.23306944
-6	-0.00332284	-0.75198054	-0.00824424	-0.54475956
-5	0.00160689	-0.10903596	-0.00663736	-0.54180891
-4	-0.00101261	0.14781393	-0.00764996	-0.44574917
-3	0.00204188	0.55775959	-0.00560809	-0.21976237
-2	0.00617540	1.01427103	0.00056731	0.13089639
-1	0.00176160	0.77918106	0.00232891	0.37057791
0	-0.00287282	-0.65311922	-0.00054392	0.15640932
1	-0.00734865	-1.63969688	-0.00789256	-0.32358920
2	-0.00547878	-0.99197415	-0.01337134	-0.58601857
3	0.00459309	0.62074066	-0.00877825	-0.39880171
4	-0.00067214	0.23380799	-0.00945039	-0.32491009
5	-0.00614908	-1.61468665	-0.01559947	-0.71826450
6	0.00105928	0.00121220	-0.01454019	-0.69652492
7	-0.00063524	-0.40914578	-0.01517543	-0.77333713
8	-0.00904202	-2.922014**	-0.02421744	-1.42306717
9	-0.00679450	-1.6882020*	-0.03101194	-1.7645277*
10	-0.00134058	-1.06535438	-0.03235252	-1.9544821*

Note: ** (*) denotes significance at the 5 (10) percent level.

Table 4.3

Test Statistics for the Portfolio of 29 U.S. Import-Competing Firms from 10 Days before to 10 Days after the Day (Day Zero) of the Settlement Agreement or Voluntary Termination of the Case

DAY	AAR	ZSPE	ACAR	ZSCPE
-10	0.00751683	2.104854**	0.00751683	1.16129885
-9	-0.00422289	-1.08976612	0.00329394	0.39601415
-8	-0.00017090	-0.71393513	0.00312304	0.09592868
-7	0.00602586	1.8116003*	0.00914890	0.58282850
-6	0.00102007	-0.77752938	0.01016897	0.32945120
-5	-0.00995730	-2.088290**	0.00021167	-0.16962097
-4	0.00033889	1.14352875	0.00055056	0.08142397
-3	0.00073239	0.02263751	0.00128295	0.08058092
-2	0.00202756	0.38884451	0.00331051	0.14748405
-1	0.00095534	1.07010003	0.00426585	0.32661653
0	-0.00190556	0.20910144	0.00236030	0.34620090
1	0.00259394	1.00788266	0.00495424	0.49198663
2	-0.00331132	0.13692404	0.00164292	0.49363768
3	0.00002331	0.63481285	0.00166623	0.56928717
4	-0.00224273	-0.85725775	-0.00057649	0.42786338
5	-0.00180164	-0.15669953	-0.00237813	0.39266321
6	0.00388225	0.81100276	0.00150412	0.48946178
7	-0.00790185	-2.398771**	-0.00639773	0.16372887
8	-0.00191802	-0.35343141	-0.00831575	0.11462668
9	0.00219404	0.24533667	-0.00612172	0.14199127
10	0.00478921	1.6434074*	-0.00133250	0.33642910

Note: ** (*) denotes significance at the 5 (10) percent level.

Table 4.4

Test Statistics for the Portfolio of 11 U.S. Import-Competing Firms from 10 Days before to 10 Days after the Day (Day Zero) of the Final USITC Negative Ruling

DAY	AAR	ZSPE	ACAR	ZSCPE
-10	0.00100533	0.14201768	0.00100533	0.20657117
-9	-0.0123063	-2.032926**	-0.01130097	-1.9448355*
-8	-0.00296557	-0.40535124	-0.01426654	-1.9283583*
-7	-0.00426946	-0.82158730	-0.01853601	-2.267525**
-6	0.00094568	-0.32124911	-0.01759033	-2.237106**
-5	-0.00362144	-0.51424242	-0.02121176	-2.347554**
-4	0.00688727	1.00744947	-0.0143245	-1.61955133
-3	0.00680184	0.78932415	-0.00752266	-1.10903413
-2	0.00302384	0.06837253	-0.00449882	-1.01245708
-1	-0.0044023	-0.74210077	-0.00890112	-1.30184348
0	0.00311962	0.36501516	-0.00578150	-1.08117730
1	-0.00226051	-0.34742346	-0.00804201	-1.18102847
2	0.00400004	0.93242197	-0.00404197	-0.75853935
3	0.00234349	0.58664972	-0.00169848	-0.50289047
4	0.01041124	1.6718223*	0.00871276	0.14203465
5	-0.00536648	-1.20223499	0.00334628	-0.2996519
6	-0.00032246	-0.2519727	0.00302382	-0.37959575
7	0.00097694	0.13880057	0.00400077	-0.32131442
8	-0.00627072	-0.99070494	-0.00226996	-0.64333838
9	0.00941506	1.54282675	0.00714510	-0.12525007
10	-0.0040754	-0.74691539	0.00306970	-0.35930835

Note: ** (*) denotes significance at the 5 (10) percent level.

which is significant at 5 percent. This may suggest that market participants can anticipate the ruling. On day 4, the AAR is 1 percent and the ZSPE is 1.67, which is significant at 10 percent. This reversal may suggest that there might be an over reaction in the earlier period. The Figure 4.2 shows that the ACAR goes down first and then up, and the gain in the later period more than offsets the loss in the earlier period. However, the ZSCPE is not significant for the whole period.

In view of all these results, we have to conclude that, in general, the unfair trade practice petitions and the subsequent outcomes do not have the impact on petition firms' stock prices as we hypothesized. The counter-intuitive results in Tables 4.1, 4.2, and 4.3 are puzzling. Since the cases are firm specific, there is no dilution problem. Therefore, it is hard to imagine why firms keep filing petitions if the petitions will not benefit but harm the petitioning firms. One possible explanation is that the sample size is too small, especially for outcome period. Another possible explanation is that the unfair trade practice petitions actually signal the weakness of the petition firms, i.e., losing competitiveness. Therefore the petition may cause negative impact on all petition firms during the petition period and negative impact for the firms with affirmative ITC rulings during the outcome period. However, it can not explain why we do not observe the positive abnormal returns for the firms with the negative ITC rulings during the outcome period. It is also possible that the effects of these events had been anticipated by market participants before the petition and outcome period, so the petition and the outcome events contain little information. According to Finger, et al. (1982), the decision process for unfair trade practice cases is more routine and thus subject to less uncertainty and relatively easy to forecast. From Table 4.1 to 4.4, we see no significant ZSPE for days -1, 0, and 1, and the most significant ZSPEs we observed are more than three days apart from day zero. Therefore, we may only have captured some noise.

4.2 Trade Deficit News and U.S. Import-Competing Firms

In Chapter 3 (section 3.2.2), we discussed the possible signals conveyed by the trade deficit news and the possible effects of the trade deficit news on stock prices. We also introduced a simple regression model, equation (3.30):

$$R_{it} = \alpha + \beta NEWS_t + \varepsilon_{it}$$

where NEWS is proxied by percentage forecast error as expressed by equation (3.12):

Trade Deficit News=(Announced Deficit - Expected Deficit)
÷ Expected Deficit

In this section, we apply equation (3.30) to test the trade deficit news effect on the U.S. stock prices. The hypothesized trade deficit news effects on the stock prices of U.S. import-competing firms and the market index summarized in Table 3.1 is reprinted in Table 4.5. If the trade deficit news had an impact on the stock prices as hypothesized in the Table, then the estimated ß should be significantly different from zero with the expected sign correspondingly.

Table 4.5

Hypothesized Trade Deficit News Signals and the Expected Signs of Their Impacts on Stock Prices

	U.S. Import-Competing Firm	U.S. Market Return
Reducing Gov't Spending	?	−
Dollar Depreciation without Inflation	+	?
Dollar Depreciation with Inflation	-	-
Increasing Protection	+	?
Losing Competitiveness	−	?

Note: + denotes positive impact; - negative; and ? ambiguous.

4.2.1 Data

Monthly trade deficit announcement figures and the corresponding forecast Figures are obtained from Money Market Service Inc. (see Appendix B). This is the same data source as used by previous researchers. The sample period runs from February 1980 to December 1988. The U.S. trade balance during this period was all in deficit, so the monthly trade balance announcement was actually the trade deficit announcement. Until February 1987, the trade deficit for month t-1 was announced in the last week of month t. Since April 1987, the trade deficit figure for month t-2 was announced in the second week of month t. From February 1980 to October 1983, the announcement time was 2:30 pm EST. In November 1983 it was 9:30 am EST. Since December 1983, it has been 8:30 am EST.

Table 4.6

U.S. Import-competing Industries and Their Corresponding Firm Numbers

Industry	Number of Firms
Textile	25
Apparel	26
Lumber & Wood	7
Non-rubber Footwear	12
Steel	28
Electronic Components	58
Car & Motorcycle	26

The U.S. import-competing firms in this study are identified according to the industries which were threatened by foreign competition. During the Reagan years, there were nine major domestic industries that had sought increased protection from Congress. They were automobiles, non-rubber footwear, textile and apparel, sugar, machine tools, steel, softwood lumber, copper, and semiconductors. Seven of these industries are identified from four-digit Standard Industry Code (SIC) and their corresponding firms listed on the NYSE, AMEX, and NASDAQ with daily returns available from the CRSP data tape are finally selected. The identified industries and the number of selected firms in each industry are shown in Table 4.6.

The portfolio return for each industry on the announcement date is computed by taking the simple arithmetic mean of the daily (close$_{t-1}$ to close$_t$) return of each firm in the industry. The portfolio return of the 58 firms involved in the unfair trade practice cases are also computed.

4.2.2 Results

Table 4.7 presents the estimation of equation (3.30) for the whole period of February 1980 to December 1988. The daily returns for seven industry portfolios, the portfolio of unfair trade practice petition firms, and the CRSP equally weighted market return are used as dependent variables and regressed on the trade deficit news. The estimated news effect, ß, is not significantly different from zero in all the regressions. The result is inconsistent with any of the hypotheses presented in Table 4.5. A reduction in U.S. aggregate expenditure may produce an insignificant effect on the stock price of import-competing firms, but should have a significant negative impact on the market return. However, as shown in Table 4.7 the estimated ß for the market return is -0.00014 with a t-value of 0.062. Considering the great concern caused by the huge U.S. trade deficit in the 1980s, the general lack of the trade deficit news effect across all portfolios seems surprising.

One possibility that might lead to this result is that the impact of trade deficit news on these portfolio returns is time-varying. It is reasonable to argue that the impact of trade deficit news on these stock returns is varying with the trade deficit level, i.e., the trade deficit news effect is larger when the trade deficit level is higher. The simplest way to model this possibility is to hypothesize a linear relationship between the news effect ß and the trade deficit level as in equation (3.31):

$$\beta_t = c + d * DEF_t$$

The reduced form equation (3.32):

$$R_{jt} = a + c * NEWS_t + d * NEWS_t * DEF_t + \varepsilon_{it}$$

Table 4.7

U.S. Monthly Trade Deficit Announcement Effects On U.S. Import-Competing Firms' Stock Prices.

OLS: $R_{it} = a_i + b_i NEWS_t + e_{it}$

i = individual industry or portfolio

t = announcement date (Feb. 1980 - Dec. 1988, 106 observations)

News = Trade deficit forecast error as a percentage of expected trade
       deficit

R = Daily stock return

R_{it}	Constant	News	R^2	# of Firms
Petition Firms	0.00014	0.00006	0.0000	6
	(0.123)	(0.022)		
Textile	0.00055	-0.00241	0.0093	25
	(0.548)	(-0.988)		
Apparel	-0.00006	0.00129	0.0023	26
	(-0.054)	(0.486)		
Lumber & Wood	0.00010	-0.00239	0.0067	7
	(0.089)	(-0.838)		
Nonrubber	0.00025	-0.00092	0.0016	12
Footware	(0.274)	(-0.411)		
Steel	-0.00118	0.00052	0.0003	28
	(-1.047)	(0.188)		
Electronic Comp.	0.00064	-0.00085	0.0006	58
	(0.474)	(-0.258)		
Car & Motorcycle	0.00028	-0.00093	0.0015	26
	(0.290)	(-0.395)		
EWMKTR	0.00016	-0.00014	0.0000	
	(0.173)	(0.062)		

Note: t statistics in parentheses.

Table 4.8

Linearly Time-Varying Trade News Effect On U.S. Import-competing Firms' Stock Prices (106 observations from Feb. 1980 to Dec. 1988)

$$R_{it} = \alpha + c * NEWS_t + d * NEWS_t * DEF_t + \varepsilon_t$$

R_{it}	Constant	NEWS	NEWS*DEF	dR/dNEWS	R^2
Petition Firms	0.00093 (0.779)	0.00850 (1.749)*	0.00160 (-2.102)**	-0.00525 (-1.241)	0.0411
Textile	0.00068 (0.637)	-0.00105 (-0.241)	0.00025 (-0.379)	0.00320 (-0.838)	0.0107
Apparel	0.00021 (0.181)	0.00417 (0.884)	0.00055 (-0.739)	-0.00056 (-0.135)	0.0075
Lumber & Wood	0.00109 (0.899)	0.00816 (1.653)*	0.00201 (-2.587)**	-0.00911 (-2.112)**	0.0670
Nonrubber Footwear	0.00065 (0.678)	0.00341 (0.863)	0.00082 (-1.326)	-0.00363 (-1.050)	0.0184
Steel	-0.00067 (-0.565)	0.00603 (1.246)	0.00105 (-1.379)	-0.00299 (-0.706)	0.0185
Electronic Comp.	0.00107 (0.750)	0.00375 (0.643)	0.00087 (-0.954)	-0.00373 (-0.729)	0.0094
Car & Motorcycle	0.00069 (0.680)	0.00349 (0.840)	0.00084 (-1.286)	-0.00373 (-1.025)	0.0173
EWMKTR	0.00056 (0.574)	0.00446 (1.111)	0.00082 -1.303)	-0.00259 (-0.737)	0.0162

Note: t statistics in parentheses; ** (*) denotes significance at the 5 (10) percent level.

which takes the linearly time-varying hypothesis into consideration is estimated in Table 4.8. Only for the lumber & wood portfolio and the petition firms portfolio do the results support a linearly time-varying ß. The coefficients of the interactive term NEWS*DEF are 0.00201 and -0.00160 respectively for the above mentioned portfolios and both are significant at the 5 percent level. The coefficients of NEWS are 0.00816 and 0.00850 and both significant at the 10 percent level.

The trade deficit news effect on the portfolio returns can be inferred from the derivative $dR_{it}/dNEWS_t = c+d*DEF_t = ß_t$. Using the coefficients reported in the Table and the mean of monthly trade deficit (8.592), we compute the mean of $ß_t$ which is presented in the last column of the Table. The standard errors are computed from the variance-covariance matrix of the estimated equation and the implied t statistics are given in parentheses. The mean of $ß_t$ for lumber & wood portfolio is -0.00911 and is significant at the 5 percent level. This suggests that the trade deficit news effect on the stock prices of the lumber & wood portfolio is linearly varying with the trade deficit level over time and, on average, the news effect is negative and significantly different from zero. In conjunction with the insignificant effect on the market return, it is consistent with the losing competitiveness hypothesis. The mean of $ß_t$ for the petition firms portfolio is -0.00525 but is not significant, which suggests that although the trade deficit news effect is linearly time-varying with the trade deficit level, the effect is not significant on average.

Another way to look at the possibility that the trade deficit news effect may change over time is to break the whole sample period into subsample periods and see whether the news effect is different across the subperiods. Both Deravi, Gregorowic, and Hegji (1988) and Hogan, Melvin and Roberts (1990) documented that trade deficit news had a negatively significant impact on foreign exchange rates in the second half of the 1980s but not in the first half. A review of *The Wall Street Journal* reveals the trade deficit announcement was interestingly omitted as a factor worth mentioning in financial asset pricing in the early years of the 1980s. On April 30, 1984, the foreign exchange column mentioned that analysts were now paying close attention to the trade account. Through the following years, the trade deficit announcement was frequently mentioned as an important determinant of exchange rates as well as stock prices. Also the biggest jump of the U.S. trade deficit occurred in 1984. As shown in

Table 1.1, the trade deficit was \$52.41 billion in 1983, but \$106.68 billion in 1984 and has stayed above \$100 billion since then. Therefore, we break the whole sample period into two subsample periods: the first one starts from February 1980 to April 1984 and the second from May 1984 to December 1988.

The estimation of equation (3.30) for the first subsample period is presented in Table 4.9, panel A, and the second subsample is in panel B. In panel A, as in Table 4.7, all the portfolio returns show no response to the trade deficit news. In panel B however, the trade deficit news had a negative impact on petition firms, lumber & wood, and electronic components portfolio returns. The estimated ßs for these portfolio returns are -0.01754, -0.01462 and -0.01130 respectively. For petition firms portfolio the ß is significant at the 5 percent level, and for the other two, the ß is significant at the 10 percent level. The above observations do suggest that the trade deficit news changes over time and this is also consistent with the assertion that market participants paid closer attention to trade deficit announcements in the second half of the 1980s. The negative sign of the three estimated ßs also lend some support to the losing competitiveness hypothesis, i.e., an unexpectedly large trade deficit signals the deteriorating competitiveness of the corresponding U.S. import-competing firms and, thus, is associated with a decrease in their stock prices.

4.3 Summary and Comments

In view of the whole results, the responses of U.S. import-competing firms' stock prices to trade related news were not strong. For protection news, the event of an unfair trade practice petition and the subsequent outcome had a vague or counter-intuitive impact on the petition firms' stock prices. The possible reasons may be that market participants had expected the events before the petition and the outcome period so that the events themselves did not contain much news content, or the sample size is too small.

For trade deficit news, the market return and five out of seven import-competing industry portfolio returns were insensitive to the trade deficit news for the whole sample period as well as for each subperiod. For the two industry portfolio returns that had a

Table 4.9

U.S. Monthly Trade Deficit Announcement Effects On U.S. Import-Competing Firms' Stock Prices.

OLS:	$R_{it} = a_i + b_i NEWS_t + e_{it}$

i = individual industry or portfolio

t = announcement date

News = Trade deficit forecast error as a percentage of expected trade deficit

R = daily stock return

Panel A (From Feb. 1980 to April 1984, 51 observations)

R_{it}	Constant	News	R^2	# of Firms
Petition Firms	-0.00074	0.00236	0.0103	62
	(-0.396)	(0.714)		
Textile	-0.00097	-0.00201	0.0110	25
	(- 0.627)	(-0.739)		
Apparel	-0.00227	0.00294	0.0181	26
	(-1.302)	(0.951)		
Lumber & Wood	-0.00088	-0.00065	0.0008	7
	(-0.470)	(-0.195)		
Nonrubber Footwear	-0.00128	0.00069	0.0016	12
	(-0.904)	(0.277)		
Steel	-0.00269	0.00242	0.0127	28
	(-1.574)	(0.795)		
Electronic Comp.	-0.00235	0.00149	0.0024	58
	(-0.958)	(0.342)		
Car & Motorcycle	0.00075	0.00051	0.0007	26
	(-0.473)	(0.183)		
EWMKTR	-0.00140	0.00176	0.0000	
	(-0.888)	(0.628)		

Table 4.9 (continued)

Panel B (From Feb. 1984 to May 1988, 55 observations)

R_{it}	Constant	News	R^2	# of Firms
Petition Firms	0.00113	-0.01754	0.0960	62
	(0.841)	(-2.372)**		
Textile	0.00185	-0.00241	0.0001	25
	(1.339)	(-0.084)		
Apparel	0.00196	0.00577	0.0117	26
	(1.478)	(-0.791)		
Lumber &	0.00112	-0.01462	0.0587	7
Wood	(0.765)	(-1.818)*		
Nonrubber	0.00171	-0.01005	0.0438	12
Footwear	(1.452)	(-1.559)		
Steel	0.00029	-0.01125	0.0438	28
	(0.196)	(-1.389)		
Electronic.	0.00339	-0.01130	0.0480	58
Comp	(2.692)**	(-1.634)*		
Car &	0.00129	-0.01026	0.0464	26
Motorcycle	(1.114)	(-1.606)		
EWMKTR	0.00164	-0.00894	0.0447	
	(1.593)	(-1.575)		

Note: t statistics in parentheses; ** (*) denotes significance at the 5 (10) percent level.

significant response in the second subperiod, the significance level is only 10 percent.

Only the petition firms portfolio return had a response which is significant at the 5 percent level in the second subperiod. There are two possible explanations for these results. First, the trade deficit news effect may be diluted by the portfolio because even the firms in these portfolios may have different exposure to foreign trade. Second, the daily data may contain too much noise so that the trade deficit news effect cannot be distinguished from the noise. Puffer's findings (1990) on the Dow Jones' response to the trade deficit news provides some support for this explanation. She documented that the

Dow Jones overnight return had a statistically significant response to the trade deficit news but not the daily return. We can further investigate this possibility in the following chapters when we examine the trade deficit news effect on the stock prices of Korean and Taiwanese firms because overnight and $open_t$-$close_t$ returns for these firms are available in the PACAP data tape.

For all three portfolio returns that had a significant response to the trade deficit news, the response was negative and only observed in the second subperiod. This finding supports both the assertion that the trade deficit news effect is time-varying and the losing competitiveness hypothesis. Previous authors documented that, during the same period the trade deficit news was associated with a depreciation of the U.S. dollar in the foreign exchange market. Although most empirical studies (section 2.4) concluded that the dollar depreciation would be associated with a positive stock price movement, theoretically, it is still possible that a depreciation would be associated with a negative stock price movement if the depreciation fostered an inflation expectation. However, the inflation expectation would affect the whole market more than it would affect the import-competing firms and this is not the case in our results. Therefore, the trade deficit news effect on the exchange rates during the second subperiod actually reinforced the support for the losing competitiveness hypothesis. Based on this conclusion, the negative significant response of petition portfolio return may further suggest that losing competitiveness would lead to protection seeking activities.

Notes

---

[1] *USITC Annual Report 1989*, Appendix B, p 51.

[2] The parameters were also estimated by using Dimson methods and the results are qualitatively the same.

V

Empirical Investigation Of Taiwanese Export-Oriented Firms

5.1 Background

"Taiwan is probably the most successful of the developing countries" (M. Shahid Alam, 1989). During 1960s and 1970s, its average annual growth rate was about 9.5 percent, and it made the transition from an agricultural economy to a newly industrialized economy. Taiwan's fast economic growth has heavily relied on exports. The export share in GNP went up from 9.6 percent in 1960 to 26.3 percent in 1970 and 48.7 percent in 1981. For most of the post-World-War-Two years, the U.S. has been Taiwan's largest export market. Exports to the U.S. as a share of its total exports have often been in the range between 50 percent and 80 percent. In the 1980s Taiwan ran a large bilateral trade surplus with the U.S.. In the second half of the 1980s, this surplus was second only to that of Japan.[1]

This large trade surplus caused increased trade conflicts between the U.S. and Taiwan in the 1980s, especially in the second half of the 1980s. During this period Taiwan was frequently named by the U.S. as an unfair trading partner, and was pressed to restrict its exports to the U.S. and open its markets for U.S. products. Considering the importance of U.S. markets to Taiwan's economy, it is expected that the possible U.S. trade restrictions against Taiwan should have affected Taiwanese export-oriented firms. In this chapter we will examine the effect of U.S -Taiwan trade conflict events and the U.S. trade deficit news on Taiwanese export-oriented firms' stock prices.

5.2 *General U.S - Taiwan Trade Conflict News Effect*

5.2.1 *Event Description*

A general U.S-Taiwan trade conflict event is an event which may produce a general impact on all the Taiwanese export-oriented firms. For example, the Reagan administration's decision to withdraw duty-free privileges from Taiwan or its pressure on Taiwan to appreciate the new Taiwanese dollar against the U.S. dollar would adversely affect all the Taiwanese export-oriented firms. On the other hand, the responses of the Taiwanese government to reduce tariffs on imports or open its markets to U.S. beer, wine, and cigarettes may ease the tension and thwart some possible U.S. retaliation. All these are considered as general conflict events.

According to this criterion, 14 general conflict events were identified from *The Wall Street Journal (WSJ)*. The first event was made public on March 28, 1984 and the last on February 2, 1988. Table 5.1 summarizes these general conflict events, their press date, and each event's expected impact on the export-oriented firms' stock prices.

5.2.2 *Data of Taiwanese Export-Oriented Firms*

The relevant firms here are not just export-oriented firms but the firms that export to the U.S. and whose exports are often threatened by possible U.S. trade restrictions. A review of the *USITC Annual Report* in the 1980s reveals that the exports from three Taiwanese industries were often the subject of complaints by U.S. firms and laborers. They were electric machinery & machinery, iron & steel, and electronic industries. Therefore, we identify these industries as the export-oriented industries and the firms in these industries with daily stock returns available on the PACAP data tape as the export-oriented firms. Table 5.2 lists these industries and the number of firms in each industry. The event day is the day that the trade conflict news appeared in the *WSJ*, which we define as day zero. We also define a two-day event period as day -1 (the day before the event day) and day zero to account for the information leakage on the day before the event day. Since Taipei time is 13 hours ahead of New

Table 5.1

Event Descriptions

This table lists 14 major U.S.-Taiwan trade conflict news items which may have had some general impact on Taiwanese export-oriented industries during the mid-1980s

Event	Date	Descriptions

1 84/03/28 The Reagan administration announced major reductions in the duty-free privileges of Taiwan, Mexico, South Korea, and other fast growing third world nations.

This event is predicted to have had a negative impact on the export-oriented firms since their price competitiveness in the U.S. markets would be hurt.

2 84/08/07 Taiwan agreed to reduce tariffs on 59 products and gradually eliminate a 10 percent import surcharge, a move that could spur U.S. exports of wood products, semi-finished leather goods, etc..

This event is predicted to have had a positive impact on the export-oriented firms since it would ease tensions between the U.S. and Taiwan.

3 84/11/27 The Taiwanese government submitted to its legislature a plan to eliminate import taxes on 35 items and scale down levies on 1058 items.

This event is predicted to have had a positive impact on the export- oriented firms since it would greatly reduce the barrier to imports and might reduce the surplus with the U.S.

4 85/10/17 Taiwan agreed to allow sales of U.S. wine, beer and cigarettes at more than 70,000 retail outlets.

Table 5.1 (Continued)

Event	Date	Descriptions
	85/10/18	Taiwan was warned by a group of visiting U.S. senators that the continuing trade surplus with the U.S. was a threat to bilateral ties.
		The two successive announcements might have had offsetting effects on the export-oriented firms and the total effect would be ambiguous.
5	86/07/28	The Reagan administration planned exchange-rate negotiations with Taiwan and South Korea in an effort to win a better break on trade; the move was ordered by Treasury Secretary James Baker, in response to mounting protectionist pressure.
		This event is predicted to have had a negative impact on the export-oriented firms since it might lead to the appreciation of the new Taiwanese dollar (NT$) against the U.S. dollar and reduce the competitiveness of Taiwanese export-oriented firms in U.S. markets.
6	86/08/11	U.S. and Taiwan were close to settling a dispute over Taiwan's new system of assessing customs duties on foreign goods.
	86/08/12	The U.S. and Taiwan resolved a dispute over the way Taiwan values its imports for tariff purposes; Taiwan agree to drop its existing customs-valuation system, which the U.S. complained artificially overvalued imports in violation of a bilateral 1979 agreement.
		This event is predicted to have had a positive impact on the export-oriented firms since it might ease tensions between the two countries.

Table 5.1 (Continued)

Event	Date	Descriptions
8	86/12/09	Taiwan tentatively agreed with the Reagan administration's demands that it limit its share of U.S. machine-tool market to levels that prevailed in the early 1980's; separately, Taiwan agreed to carry out an accord to open its domestic markets to more U.S-made beer, wine and cigarettes.
		This event is predicted to have had a positive impact on the export-oriented firms since it might ease tensions between the two countries.
9	87/04/03	President Reagan withdrew duty-free privileges on more than $4 billion in annual imports from developing countries in the largest rollback by a U.S. president; Taiwan was hardest hit, losing $1.6 billion in tariff exemptions.
		This event is predicted to have had a negative impact on the export-oriented firms since they would lose $1.6 billion in tariff exemptions.
10	87/04/20	Taiwan informed the Reagan administration that it is taking steps to reduce its trade surplus with the U.S. while narrowing its trade deficit with Japan.
		This event is predicted to have had an ambiguous impact on the export-oriented firms. If the steps were import liberation, the event might have had a positive impact, and if the steps were voluntary export restriction, the event might have had a negative impact.
11	87/06/05	Taiwanese cabinet approved tariff reductions on a further 330 products as part of an effort to boost imports and lessen trade tensions.

Table 5.1 (Continued)

Event	Date	Descriptions
		This event is predicted to have had a positive impact on the export-oriented firms since it might lessen trade tensions.
12	87/06/16	Taiwan announced plans to buy 10 U.S. long-haul aircraft, valued at $1.7 billion, to narrow its trade surplus; Taiwan also announced the planned purchase $430 million of U.S. agricultural products and $180 million in industrial goods. This event is predicted to have had a positive impact on export-oriented firms since it would narrow Taiwan's trade surplus with the U.S.
13	87/10/10	Taiwan announced plans to reduce tariffs on more than 3,500 kinds of imported goods in an effort to liberalize the local market and meet calls from the U.S. and Europe for a narrowing in its surplus. This event is predicted to have had a positive impact on export-oriented firms since it might ease tensions between Taiwan and many western countries.
14	88/02/04	Taiwan and Korea, seeking to ease frictions with the U.S. and other trading partners, plan fresh measures to curb their surplus. The impact of this event is ambiguous; depending on the measures (import liberalization or voluntary export restriction) taken.

Table 5.2
Taiwanese Export-Oriented Industries and Firm Numbers

Industry	Number of Firms
Electric Machinery & Machinery	3
Electronic	7
Steel	1

York Time, as indicated in Figure 5.1, the trading time in Taiwan does not overlap with trading time in New York and the date that the trade conflict event appeared in the *WSJ*, day zero, is actually day -1 in Taipei. The sample period runs from 200 days prior to the first event (March 28, 1984) to 20 days after the last event (February 4, 1988).

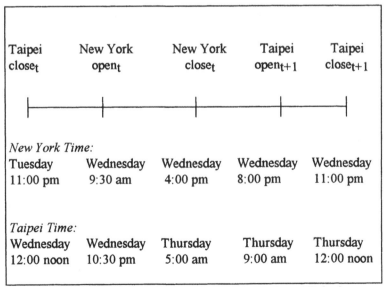

Taipei	New York	New York	Taipei	Taipei
close$_t$	open$_t$	close$_t$	open$_{t+1}$	close$_{t+1}$

New York Time:

Tuesday	Wednesday	Wednesday	Wednesday	Wednesday
11:00 pm	9:30 am	4:00 pm	8:00 pm	11:00 pm

Taipei Time:

Wednesday	Wednesday	Thursday	Thursday	Thursday
12:00 noon	10:30 pm	5:00 am	9:00 am	12:00 noon

Figure 5.1 The Time Difference between New York and Taipei

5.2.3 Measuring Trade Conflict News Effect

We use the modified version of the market model (SUR) discussed in section 3.3.2 to measure the trade conflict news effect on Taiwanese export-oriented firms' stock returns, because here we have both the event date clustering and the risk clustering. These firms are grouped into three portfolios according to the industry. The portfolio returns are computed by taking the simple average of the returns of individual firms in the portfolio.

In this case, the system of seemingly unrelated equations (3.24)

$$R_{jt} = \alpha_j + \beta_{j1}R_{mt-2} + \beta_{j2}R_{mt-1} + \beta_{j3}R_{mt} + \beta_{j4}R_{mt+1} + \beta_{j5}R_{mt+2} + \sum_{k=1}^{k} \gamma_{jk}D_{kt} + \varepsilon_{jk}$$

consists of three equations, $j = 1, 2, 3$, one for each portfolio. 14 dummy variables, $K = 14$, in each equation are used to capture the effects of the 14 events respectively. The dummy equals 1 during the corresponding two-day or one-day event period and 0 otherwise. The coefficients, γ_{jk}, multiplying the event dummy variables measure the event period average abnormal returns. The leads and lags of the market return are used to adjust for non-synchronous trading.

Two joint hypotheses about the abnormal returns during the event period can be formulated within the framework discussed in section 3.3.2. An advantage of SUR methodology is the ability to do joint hypothesis testing since heteroscedasticity across equations and contemporaneous dependence of the disturbances are explicitly incorporated into the hypothesis test. The residual returns of export-oriented industry portfolios may well exhibit heteroscedasticity and contemporaneous dependence since the variance of the residual returns across industry portfolios is generally different and it is very possible that even a general trade conflict event may benefit some industries and hurt others. Based on F-statistics defined by equation (3.27), the first null hypothesis we want to test is

$$H_0^1: \sum_{j=1}^{3} \gamma_{jk} = 0$$

The sum of the dummy variable parameters across equations for an event reflects a total influence of the event on all the portfolios, similar to the sample-wide abnormal return computed in the market model event study. The rejection of the null indicates the event had an impact on the export-oriented firms as a whole. The second hypothesis (3.28) we want to test is

$$H_0^2 : \gamma_{jk} = 0 \quad \forall j$$

This joint hypothesis can detect the effects of an event when some portfolios gain and others lose.

The SUR system (3.24) is estimated by using daily returns from 200 days prior to the first event and 20 days after the last event. Since the events occurred between early 1984 to early 1988, we have 1288 observations.

5.2.4 Results

Table 5.3 and 5.4 present the results of the SUR analysis for the two-day event period. Table 5.3 shows the two-day average abnormal returns and t-statistics for each of the 14 events across the three industry portfolios. The abnormal returns are insignificant for most events. However, four events produced significant abnormal returns for individual portfolios. Event 10 (Taiwan was taking steps to reduce its trade surplus with the U.S) produced a 1.2 percent abnormal return for the electric machinery & machinery portfolio and it is significant at the 5 percent level[2]($t = 2.262$). Event 13 (Taiwan Planned to reduce tariff on more than 3,500 kinds of imported goods), produced a 0.9 percent abnormal return for the electronic portfolio and it is significant at the 5 percent level. Event 7 and 14 produced significant (at the 1 percent level) abnormal stock returns for the steel portfolio. Event 7 (The U.S. was preparing to restrict imports from Taiwan) caused an average of 3.9 percent decrease ($t = -2.592$) in stock returns during the two-day period. Event 14 (Taiwan sought to ease friction with the U.S. and European trading partners and planned fresh measures to curb its surplus) caused an average of 4.4 percent return decrease ($t = -2.899$). The positive abnormal returns associated with event 10 and 13 are consistent with the prediction that they would ease tensions between Taiwan and U.S.

Table 5.3

Taiwanese Export-Oriented Industries' Abnormal Returns Around the Information Release of the Trade Conflict Between Taiwan and the U.S., Averaged over Days -1 through 0, Where Day 0 Is the WSJ Announcement Date.

SUR:

$$R_{it} = \beta_{i0} + \beta_{i1}R_{mt-2} + \beta_{i2}R_{mt-1} + \beta_{i3}R_{mt} + \beta_{i4}R_{mt+1} + \beta_{i5}R_{mt+2} + \sum_{k=1}^{k} a_{ik}D_{kt} + e_{it}$$

i = Individual Industry

t = 200 days prior to the first event to 20 days after the last event, altogether 1288 days.

K = 14, there are 14 events.

Event	Elec & Mach n=3	Elec Prod n=7	Steel n=1
Dum1	0.00051 (0.098)	0.00242 (0.573)	0.00981 (0.655)
Dum2	0.00399 (0.770)	0.00379 (0.899)	0.00170 (0.114)
Dum3	0.00550 (1.060)	0.00658 (1.561)	-0.00248 (-0.165)
Dum4	0.00596 (1.149)	0.00320 (0.758)	-0.02147 (-1.433)
Dum5	0.00511 (0.982)	-0.00320 (-0.758)	-0.01234 (-0.821)
Dum6	-0.00433 (-0.835)	0.00610 (1.448)	-0.00566 (-0.378)
Dum7	0.00819 (1.578)	-0.00715 (-1.695)	-0.03886 (-2.592)**
Dum8	-0.00130 (-0.250)	0.00372 (0.881)	0.01292 (0.861)

Table 5.3 continued

Event	Elec & Mach n=3	Elec Prod n=7	Steel n=1
Dum9	-0.00146 (-0.281)	0.00465 (1.100)	-0.02759 (-1.838)
Dum10	0.01185 (2.262)*	0.00044 (0.103)	0.00559 (0.370)
Dum11	0.00013 (0.025)	-0.00167 (-0.394)	0.00015 (0.010)
Dum12	0.00250 (0.482)	0.00115 (0.272)	0.00196 (0.131)
Dum13	0.00296 (0.558)	0.00916 (2.124)*	0.01255 (0.819)
Dum14	-0.00004 (-0.007)	-0.00788 (-1.865)	-0.04353 (-2.899)**

Note: t statistics in parentheses. * significant at the 5 percent level, ** significant at the 1 percent level.

Table 5.4
Joint Hypothesis Tests For Taiwanese Export-Oriented Industries

Event	$H_0^1: \sum_{1=1}^{3} a_{ik} = 0$ $F(1, 3804)$	$H_0^2: a_{ik} = 0 \ \forall_1$ $F(3, 3804)$
Dum1	0.5848	0.2472
Dum2	0.3250	0.3475
Dum3	0.3324	0.9067
Dum4	0.5463	1.1094
Dum5	0.3903	0.9690
Dum6	0.0546	1.5468
Dum7	5.1487*	4.6854**
Dum8	0.8464	0.5943
Dum9	2.1405	1.8577
Dum10	1.1312	2.0435
Dum11	0.0069	0.0640
Dum12	0.1133	0.0893
Dum13	2.0978	1.7099
Dum14	9.5017**	3.5492**

Note: * denotes significance at the 5 percent level and ** at the 1 percent level.

Table 5.5

Taiwanese Exported-Oriented Industries' Abnormal Returns on Day - 1, the Day before the Trade Conflict News Made Public.

SUR:

$$R_{it} = \beta_{i0} + \beta_{i1} R_{mt-2} + \beta_{i2} R_{mt-1} + \beta_{i3} R_{mt} + \beta_{i4} R_{mt+1} + \beta_{i5} R_{mt+2} +$$

$$\sum_{k=1}^{k} a_{ik} D_{kt} + e_{it}$$

i = Individual Industry

t = 200 days prior to the first event to 20 days after the last event, altogether 1288 days.

K = 14, there are 14 events.

Event	Elec & Mach n=3	Electric n=7	Steel n=1
Dum1	-0.00187 (-0.230)	0.00464 (0.778)	0.01418 (0.669)
Dum2	0.00609 (0.830)	0.00445 (0.747)	-0.00069 (-0.033)
Dum3	0.00692 (0.942)	0.00999 (1.676)	-0.00104 (-0.049)
Dum4	0.00164 (o.224)	0.00339 (0.569)	-0.02481 (-1.170)
Dum5	0.00231 (0.315)	-0.00785 (-1.317)	0.00311 (0.147)
Dum6	-0.00610 (-0.831)	0.00525 (0.881)	-0.04067 (-1.917)
Dum7	0.01653 (2.249)*	-0.00636 (-1.065)	-0.04421 (-2.083)*
Dum8	-0.00416 (-0.566)	0.00784 (1.313)	0.02843 (1.339)

Table 5.5 (Continued)

Event	Elec & Mach n=3	Electric n=7	Steel n=1
Dum9	0.00001 (0.002)	0.00898 (1.505)	-0.03636 (-1.714)
Dum10	-0.00604 (-0.815)	-0.00115 (-0.191)	0.00990 (0.462)
Dum11	-0.00782 (-1.056)	-0.001185 (-0.307)	0.02505 (1.171)
Dum12	0.00167 (0.227)	0.00266 (0.445)	-0.01946 (-0.917)
Dum13	-0.00465 (-0.625)	0.01186 (1.964)	0.00078 (0.036)
Dum14	-0.00218 (-0.296)	-0.00958 (-1.604)	-0.03635 (-1.712)

Note: t statistics in parentheses. * significant at the 5 percent level, ** significant at the 1 percent level.

Table 5.6

Taiwanese Exported-Oriented Industries' Abnormal Returns on Day 0, the Day the Trade Conflict News Was Made Public.

SUR:

$$R_{it} = \beta_{i0} + \beta_{i1} R_{mt-2} + \beta_{i2} R_{mt-1} + \beta_{i3} R_{mt} + \beta_{i4} R_{mt+1} + \beta_{i5} R_{mt+2} +$$

$$\sum_{k=1}^{k} a_{ik} D_{kt} + e_{it}$$

i = Individual Industry

t = 200 days prior to the first event to 20 days after the last event, altogether 1288 days.

K = 14, there are 14 events.

Event	Elec & Mach n=3	Electric n=7	Steel n=1
Dum1	0.00259	0.00022	0.00568
	(0.355)	(0.036)	(0.268)
Dum2	0.00186	0.00311	0.00432
	(0.255)	(0.520)	(0.203)
Dum3	0.00407	0.00303	-0.00378
	(0.556)	(0.505)	(-0.178)
Dum4	0.01028	0.00294	-0.01780
	(1.408)	(0.491)	(-0.839)
Dum5	0.00777	0.00162	-0.02781
	(1.061)	(0.270)	(-1.306)
Dum6	-0.00259	0.00689	0.02958
	(-0.355)	(1.150)	(1.393)
Dum7	0.00003	-0.00808	-0.03355
	(0.004)	(-1.345)	(-1.576)
Dum8	0.00159	-0.00038	-0.00244
	(0.217)	(-0.064)	(-0.115)

Table 5.6 (Continued)

Event	Elec & Mach n=3	Electric n=7	Steel n=1
Dum9	-0.00290 (-0.397)	0.00022 (0.036)	-0.01827 (-0.860)
Dum10	0.02975 (4.033)**	0.00191 (0.315)	0.00116 (0.054)
Dum11	0.00820 (1.111)	-0.00175 (-0.289)	-0.02511 (-1.172)
Dum12	0.00323 (0.442)	-0.00033 (-0.055)	0.02376 (1.118)
Dum13	0.01032 (1.394)	0.00605 (0.996)	0.02397 (1.115)
Dum14	0.00004 (0.284)	-0.00622 (-1.038)	-0.05019 (-2.362)*

Note: t statistics in parentheses. * significant at the 5 percent level, ** significant at the 1 percent level.

Table 5.7
Joint Hypothesis Tests For Taiwanese Export-Oriented Industries

Event	$H_0^1: \sum_{l=1}^{3} a_{ik} = 0$ F(1, 3804)	$H_0^2: a_{ik} = 0 \; \forall_1$ F(3, 3804)
Panel A for Day -1:		
Dum1	0.5266	0.4255
Dum2	0.1742	0.3024
Dum3	0.4519	0.9746
Dum4	0.7012	0.5838
Dum5	0.0106	0.8614
Dum6	3.0887	2.2242
Dum7	2.0730	4.1760**
Dum8	1.8426	1.4873
Dum9	1.3429	2.0012
Dum10	0.0129	0.2784
Dum11	0.4171	0.7718
Dum12	0.4099	0.3559
Dum13	0.1116	2.0244
Dum14	4.1399*	1.7856
Panel B for Day 0:		
Dum1	0.1298	0.0764
Dum2	0.1556	0.1044
Dum3	0.0198	0.1453
Dum4	0.0378	0.8387
Dum5	0.6067	0.8785
Dum6	2.0630	1.2302
Dum7	3.0954	1.4446
Dum8	0.0027	0.0266
Dum9	0.7885	0.3406
Dum10	1.8998	6.0436**
Dum11	0.6144	0.9665
Dum12	1.2758	0.5432
Dum13	2.8506	1.2123
Dum14	5.3015*	2.2582

Note: * denotes significance at the 5 percent level and ** at the 1 percent level.

and many other western countries. The negative abnormal return associated with event 7 is also consistent with the prediction because U.S. import restrictions against Taiwan may hurt Taiwanese export-oriented firms. The negative abnormal return associated with event 14 is not inconsistent with the prediction because the impact of the event depends on the concrete measures taken (see Table 5.1).

Table 5.4 shows the F-statistics for the two joint hypotheses tests. The nulls are rejected both for event 7 and event 14 at a 1 percent level. The rejection of the second hypothesis indicates that event 7 and event 14 at least have an impact on one of the three portfolios. The rejection of the first hypothesis indicates that event 7 and event 14 have an impact on the export-oriented firms as a whole.

Tables 5.5, 5.6, and 5.7 further present the estimation results of the equation (3.24) for day -1, day 0, and the joint hypothesis tests separately. In table 5.5, the significant abnormal returns are only found for event 7. It is a negative 4.4 percent for the steel portfolio but positive 1.6 percent for the electric machinery & machinery. Both are significant at the 5 percent level (t = -2.083 and t = 2.249 respectively).

In Table 5.6, the significant abnormal returns are found for event 10 on electric machinery & machinery portfolio and for event 14 on the steel portfolio. The abnormal return is 3 percent for event 10, which is significant at 1 percent (t = 4.033) , and negative 5 percent for event 14, which is significant at 5 percent (t = -2.362). Comparing the results across Tables 5.3, 5.5, and 5.6, it seems that the impact of event 7 was mainly captured on day -1, while the impacts of event 10 and 14 were mainly captured on day 0. Similar to the two-day results, event 7 caused a negative abnormal return for steel portfolio on day -1, but in addition to that, it also caused a positive abnormal return for electric machinery & machinery portfolio on day -1, and the positive abnormal return is not consistent with the prediction. For event 10, the impact is significant on the electric machinery & machinery portfolio on day 0 but not on day -1. In general, the significance level is higher for the two-day period average abnormal return than for any single-day abnormal return. In Table 5.7, it is shown that the first null hypothesis can not be rejected for all events on either day except event 14 at 5 percent significance, and the second hypothesis can be rejected only for event 7 on day -1 and event 10 on day 0, both are significant at the 1 percent level. Compared with the results shown in Table 5.4, we again find that for event 7 and 14, the two-day event period shows a higher statistical significance level of the general trade conflict news effect than either of the two single day periods. However, for event 10, while day 0 captures some effect, the two-day period does not. Considering that some of these 14 events might have been anticipated before their press date, the results here lend some support to our general hypothesis that the U.S -Taiwan trade conflict event would influence stock prices of Taiwanese export-oriented firms. In conjunction with the t-statistics shown in Tables 5.3, 5.5, and 5.6, we can also conclude that the trade conflict news effect is unequal across the industry portfolios, i.e., the general trade conflict news effect is not that general.

5.3 Specific U.S - Taiwan Trade Conflict News Effect

A specific U.S-Taiwan trade conflict event is an event which will mainly affect one Taiwanese export-oriented industry. In June 1983, some U.S. firms filed petitions with the ITC and the Commerce Department complaining that Korean and Taiwanese firms were dumping color-TV sets in U.S. markets. The ITC and the Commerce Department subsequently investigated and ruled in favor of the petitioners and the anti-dumping duty was levied on the color-TV sets imported from these two countries. During the period 1983-1984, four news items concerning this case were identified from the *WSJ*, and they are considered as specific U.S-Taiwan trade conflict events. Table 5.8 summarizes the four events, their press date, and the predicted impacts on the Taiwanese color-TV set producers.

The daily stock returns of the three major Taiwanese color-TV set producers in this period are obtained from the PACAP data tape. The three firms are Tatung, Sampo, and Kolin. The daily returns of 200 days prior to the first event to 20 days after the last event, altogether 458 observations, are used to estimate the three-equation system (equation (20)). The two-day event period is defined as day -1 and day 0, and the same two joint hypotheses described in section 5.2.3 are tested.

Table 5.9 presents the results of the SUR analysis. Panel A shows the two-day average abnormal returns for the three firms and the t-statistics. For Sampo and Kolin, no event had any impact on their stock returns. However, for Tatung, event 3 (anti-dumping duties

Table 5.8

Event Descriptions

This table lists 4 U.S. trade restriction events concerning imports of color-TV sets from South Korea and Taiwan between 1983-1984 and their expected impacts on Taiwanese color-TV set producers.

Event	Date	Descriptions
1	83/06/10	The U.S. International Trade Commission ruled that imports of Color-TV sets from South Korea and Taiwan may be harming U.S. producers.
		This event is predicted to have had a negative impact on Taiwanese color-TV firms since it increased the probability of imposing trade restrictions against these firms' exports to the U.S. markets.
2	83/10/13	U.S. Commerce Department ruled South Korea and Taiwan were exporting color-TV sets in the U.S. at unfairly low prices in violation of the anti-dumping act.
		This event is predicted to have had a negative impact on Taiwanese color-TV set producers since it further increased the probability of imposing trade restrictions against these firms exports to the U.S. markets.
3	84/02/27	A government finding that some South Korea and Taiwanese firms were selling color-TV sets in the U.S. at below home market prices may lead to the imposition of anti-dumping duties.
		This event is predicted to have had a negative impact on Taiwanese color-TV set producers since it further increased the probability of imposing trade restrictions against these firms exports to the U.S. markets.

Table 5.8 (Continued)

Event	Date	Descriptions
4	84/04/06	The U.S. International Trade Commission ruled that imports of color-TV sets from South Korea and Taiwan were injuring domestic producers. This event is predicted to have had a negative impact on the color- TV set producers since the anti-dumping duty on color-TV sets imported from Taiwan would be unavoidable.

may be imposed on color-TV sets imported from Taiwan) had a negative significant impact on its stock prices. The two-day average abnormal return is negative 1.7 percent, which is significant at the 5 percent level ($t = -2.36$). This negative impact is consistent with the prediction that the U.S. trade restriction aimed at Taiwanese firms would produce a negative impact on their stock prices. The result that event 3 only influenced Tatung but not Sampo and Kolin may be explained by the fact that Tatung is the largest color-TV set producer and thus may be the largest exporter. It is also said that both Sampo and Kolin produced mainly for the domestic market during that period. However, we can not get the relevant data to confirm this explanation. The lack of responses to the first two events may be due to the fact that the rulings associated with these events were preliminary and subject to changes later. The event 4 (the final ITC ruling to imposing anti-dumping duty) was already expected (see event 3), so that no significant abnormal return is generated.

Panel B shows the F-statistics for the two joint hypotheses tests. The first null hypothesis that the sum of the dummy coefficients for each event across equations equals zero can not be rejected for all four events, which indicates the events had no impact on the three firms as a whole. The second null hypothesis that the kth event had no impact on each firm is rejected for event 3 at the 5 percent significance level but not for the other events. This is consistent with the above finding that the response to event 3 is firm specific. Tables 5.10 and 5.11 further present the estimation results for day -1 and day 0 separately. Basically, the results are not very much different from

Table 5.9

Taiwanese TV-Set Export Firms' Abnormal Returns Averaged over Days -1 through 0, Where Day 0 Is the *WSJ* Announcement Date, and the F-statistics.

Panel A

SUR:

$$R_{it} = \beta_{i0} + \beta_{i1}R_{mt-2} + \beta_{i2}R_{mt-1} + \beta_{i3}R_{mt} + \beta_{i4}R_{mt+1} + \beta_{i5}R_{mt+2} +$$

$$\sum_{k=1}^{k} a_{ik}D_{kt} + e_{it}$$

i = individual firm (1,2,3)

t = 200 days prior to the first event date to 20 days after the last event date, altogether 458 observations.

$K = 4$, there are 4 events.

Event	Tatung	Sampo	Kolin
Dum1	0.00192	0.00022	0.00156
	(0.263)	(-0.026)	(-0.207)
Dum2	0.00028	0.00965	0.00114
	(-0.038)	(-1.132)	(-0.141)
Dum3	0.01743	0.00579	0.00716
	(-2.360)**	(-0.672)	(0.941)
Dum4	0.00125	0.00251	0.00175
	(-0.171)	(0.295)	(0.233)

Panel B	Hypothesis Tests	
	$H_0^1: \sum_{i=1}^{3} a_{ik} = 0$	$H_0^2: a_{ik} = 0, \forall i$
Event	F(1, 1344)	F(4, 1344)
Dum1	0.0001	0.0548
Dum2	0.3568	0.5855
Dum3	0.7450	2. 9424**
Dum4	0.0120	0.0949

Note: t statistics in parentheses in panel A; **(*) denotes significance at 5 (10) percent.

Table 5.10

Taiwanese TV-Set Export Firms' Abnormal Returns on Day -1, the Day before the News Made Public.

Panel A

SUR:

$$R_{it} = \beta_{i0} + \beta_{i1}R_{mt-2} + \beta_{i2}R_{mt-1} + \beta_{i3}R_{mt} + \beta_{i4}R_{mt+1} + \beta_{i5}R_{mt+2} + \sum_{k=1}^{k} a_{ik}D_{kt} + e_{it}$$

i = individual firm (1,2,3)

t = 200 days prior to the first event date to 20 days after the last event date, altogether 458 observations.

$K = 4$, there are 4 events.

Event	Tatung	Sampo	Kolin
Dum1	0.00338	0.00663	-0.00234
	(0.327)	(0.551)	(-0.220)
Dum2	-0.00838	-0.00877	-0.01428
	(-0.810)	(-0.726)	(-1.345)
Dum3	-0.01762	0.00255	0.00257
	(-1.691)*	(0.209)	(0.240)
Dum4	0.00645	0.00316	0.01098
	(0.625)	(0.262)	(1.036)

Panel B

Hypothesis Tests

Event	$H_0^1: \sum_{l=1}^{3} a_{lk} = 0$	$H_0^1: a_{lk} = 0 \ \forall_l$
	F(1, 1344)	F(4, 1344)
Dum1	0.0875	0.2132
Dum2	1.4626	0.6622
Dum3	0.2285	1.4189
Dum4	0.6304	0.4546

Note: t statistics in parentheses in panel A; **(*) denotes significance at 5 (10) percent.

Table 5.11

Taiwanese TV-Set Export Firms' Abnormal Returns on Day 0, the Day the News Made Public.

SUR:

$$R_{it} = \beta_{i0} + \beta_{i1}R_{mt-2} + \beta_{i2}R_{mt-1} + \beta_{i3}R_{mt} + \beta_{i4}R_{mt+1} + \beta_{i5}R_{mt+2} +$$

$$\sum_{k=1}^{k} a_{ik}D_{kt} + e_{it}$$

i = individual firm (1,2,3)

t = 200 days prior to the first event date to 20 days after the last event date, altogether 458 observations.

$K = 4$, there are 4 events.

Panel A

Event	Tatung	Sampo	Kolin
Dum1	0.00060	-0.00689	-0.00082
	(0.058)	(-0.573)	(-0.078)
Dum2	0.00786	-0.01056	0.01216
	(0.759)	(-0.876)	(1.144)
Dum3	-0.01691	-0.01398	0.01162
	(-1.626)*	(-1.154)	(1.089)
Dum4	-0.00902	-0.00827	-0.00744
	(-0.873)	(-0.687)	(-0.701)

Panel B

Hypothesis Tests

Event	$H_0^1: \sum_{i=1}^{3} a_{ik} = 0$	$H_0^2: a_{ik} = 0, \forall i$
	F(1, 1344)	F(4, 1344)
Dum1	0.0750	0.1671
Dum2	0.1321	1.7820
Dum3	0.5430	2,3688*
Dum4	0.9061	0.3286

Note: t statistics in parentheses in panel A; **(*) denotes significance at 5 (10) percent.

Table 5.12

Hypothesized Trade Deficit News Signals and the Expected Signs of
Their Impacts on Stock Prices

Stock Return Response	Taiwanese Export-Oriented Firms
Reducing U.S. Spending	-
Dollar Depreciation without Inflation	-
Dollar Depreciation with Inflation	+
Increasing U.S. Protection	-
Losing U.S Competitiveness	+

Note: + denotes positive impact; - negative.

that shown in Table 5.9 except the significance level. It is significant
at the 5 percent level for Tatung in Table 5.9, but only significant at
the 10 percent level for Tatung on both day -1 and day 0. Also for day
-1, none of the null joint hypotheses can be rejected. It seems to
suggest that the two-day period can capture trade conflict effects
better.

5.4 U.S. Trade Deficit News Effect

The equation (3.30) is used to examine the trade deficit news
effect on Taiwanese export-oriented firms. The trade deficit news
data are the same as that used in section 4.2 and the export-oriented
firms are the same as those listed in Table 5.2. The dependent
variables used in the regression are daily exchange rate change, the
daily and intra-daily portfolio returns, and the daily equally weighted
market returns (EWMKTR) around the trade deficit announcement.
The intra-daily returns are the overnight (close$_{t-1}$ to open$_t$) return and
the trading time (open$_t$ to close$_t$) return. For the whole sample period
(February, 1980 to December 1988) the trade deficit announcement
came when the Taipei Stock Exchange was closed (see figure 5.1)

and there are 98 observations during this period. The portfolio return is the simple average of the firm returns in the portfolio. The hypothesized trade deficit effects on the export-oriented portfolio returns are summarized in Table 5.12.

We expect that the U.S. trade deficit news effect on EWMKTR would have been insignificant because of the "watering down" effect, however, if it was not watered down by non-trade related firms, the expected sign of the effect should be the same as that shown for the export-oriented firms. Since for most of the period under investigation, the New Taiwanese Dollar (NT$) was pegged to the US$, the trade deficit news is expected to have had no impact on the NT$/US$ exchange rate.

Table 5.13 presents the estimation results of equation (3.30) for the whole sample period. As expected, the trade deficit news had no impact on NT$/US$ exchange rate and the market return. However, two out of three portfolios had significant responses to the trade deficit news. For the electric machinery & machinery portfolio, the response occurred in the overnight (close$_{t-1}$ to open$_t$) return and the corresponding ß is -0.00418 which is significant at the 10 percent level (t = -1.671). For the electronic portfolio the response occurred in the trading time (open$_t$ to close$_t$) return as well as the daily (close$_{t-1}$ to close$_t$) return. For the trading time return the ß is -0.00542 which is significant at the 10 percent level (t = -1.731) and for the daily return, the ß is -0.00848 which is significant at the 5 percent level (t = -2.318). This suggests that the daily return, which is the cumulative of the two intra-daily returns, captured more of the trade deficit news than any one of the intra-daily returns.

Table 5.14 presents the estimation results of equation (3.32) which tests the linearly time-varying trade deficit news effect hypothesis. The results of electric machinery & machinery portfolio and electronic portfolio lend some support for the hypothesis that the trade deficit news effect is linearly time-varying with the trade deficit level. For the overnight returns of both portfolios, the estimated coefficients of interactive terms NEWS*DEF are -0.00151 and -0.00175 respectively and both are significant at the 5 percent level (t = -1.977 and -2.473 respectively). The calculated means of the corresponding ß$_t$ are shown in the last column of the table. It is -0.00925 for electric machinery & machinery portfolio and -0.00951 for electronic portfolio, but both are insignificant. This indicates that the trade deficit news effect is linearly time-varying for these two portfolios but on average the effect is insignificant.

Table 5.15 presents the estimation results of equation (3.30) for the two subsample periods. Panel A shows the results for the period from February, 1980 to April, 1984. Only the electronic portfolio shows the response to the trade deficit news. The estimated ß for the daily return is -0.00761 and for the trading time return -0.00683, and both are significant at the 5 percent level (t = -2.325 and -2.414 respectively). Panel B shows the results for the period from May 1984 to December, 1988. Similar to the results for the whole sample period, both the electric machinery & machinery portfolio and electronic portfolio show significant responses to the trade deficit news and the responses are concentrated on overnight returns. For the electric machinery & machinery portfolio, the ß is -0.02398 and for the electronic portfolio -0.02406, and both are significant at the 5 percent level (t = -2.204 and -2.366).

Based on the above results, we can make the following inferences. First, the trade deficit news had no impact on the exchange rate during the whole sample period as well as during each of the subsample periods, which is consistent with the fact the NT$ was pegged to the US$ in most of the 1980s. Therefore, we can rule out the possibility that the trade deficit news could have affected the export-oriented firms via its impact on the exchange rate changes. Second, the trade deficit news had no impact on the Taiwanese equally weighted stock market return during the whole sample period as well as each of the subsample periods but had an impact on two out of the three export-oriented industry portfolios. This confirms our belief that the trade deficit news effect on the market return is watered down by the non-trade related firms. Third, the trade deficit news effect on the electric machinery & machinery portfolio and the electronic portfolio are negative. Since the possibilities that the trade deficit news signaled the reduced U.S. government spending and exchange rate changes were ruled out (see Section 4.2 and Table 5.13), we conclude that the results in this section support the protection hypothesis, i.e., a larger than expected U.S. trade deficit increased the probability of raising protection against the Taiwanese export-oriented firms. Finally, the results shown in this section support the hypothesis that the trade deficit news effect was time varying. The trade deficit news effect in the second subperiod is stronger than that in either the first subperiod or the whole sample

Table 5.13

U.S. Monthly Trade Deficit Announcement Effects On NT$/US$ Exchange Rate and Taiwanese Export-Oriented Firms' Stock Prices For The Whole Sample Period (Feb. 1980 to Dec. 1988).

OLS:	$R_{it} = a_i + b_i NEWS_t + e_{it}$

i = Individual Portfolio.

t = Announcement date (98 observations).

News = Trade deficit forecast error (%)

R_i = Daily exchange rate change or stock return.

R_{it}	Constant	News	R^2	# of Firm
Exchange Rate Change				
$Close_{t-1} - Close_t$	-0.00698	0.00716	0.0136	
	(-2.614)**	(1.138)		
Electric & Machinary				3
$Close_{t-1} - Close_t$	0.01188	0.00124	0.0021	
	(10.129)**	(0.444)		
$Close_{t-1} - Open_t$	0.00060	0.00418	0.0283	
	(0.566)	(-1.671)*		
$Open_t - Close_t$	0.01021	0.00158	0.0033	
	(8.708)**	(0.566)		
Electric Products				7
$Close_{t-1} - Close_t$	0.00141	-0.00848	0.0530	
	(0.916)	(-2.318)**		
$Close_{t-1} - Open_t$	0.00093	0.00361	0.0242	
	(0.944)	(-1.543)		
$Open_t - Close_t$	0.00042	-0.00542	0.0303	
	(0.318)	(-1.731)*		
Iron & Steel				1
$Close_{t-1} - Close_t$	0.00012	-0.00630	0.0122	
	(0.047)	(-1.068)		
$Close_{t-1} - Open_t$	0.00295	-0.00536	0.0049	
	(0.866)	(-0.675)		
$Open_t - Close_t$	-0.00247	-0.00065	0.0002	
	(-1.075)	(-0.121)		
EWMKTR				
$Close_{t-1} - Close_t$	0.00060	-0.00483	0.0225	
	(0.437)	(-1.486)		

Note: t statistics in parentheses; ** (*) denotes significance at the 5 (10) percent level.

Table 5.14

Linearly Time-Varying Trade News Effect On Taiwanese Export-Oriented Firms' Stock Returns (98 observations from Feb. 1980 to Dec. 1988)

$$R_{it} = \alpha + c * NEWS_t + d * NEWS_t DEF_t + \varepsilon_{it}$$

Stock Return	Constant	NEWS	NEWS*DEF	dR/dNEWS	R^2
Electric & Machinary					
$Close_{t-1}$ - $Close_t$	0.01227	0.00533	-0.00080	-0.00144	0.0110
	(9.874)**	(1.021)	(-0.927)	(-0.025)	
$Close_{t-1}$ - $Open_t$	0.00132	0.00352	-0.00151	-0.00925	0.0667
	(1.204)	(0.763)	(-1.977)**	(-0.169)	
$Open_t$ - $Close_t$	0.01037	0.00320	0.00032	0.00049	0.0047
	(8.290)**	(0.611)	(-0.367)	(0.008)	
Electric Products					
$Close_{t-1}$ - $Close_t$	0.00155	-0.00695	0.00030	-0.00948	0.0537
	(0.947)	(-1.012)	(-0.263)	(-0.123)	
$Close_{t-1}$ - $Open_t$	0.00177	0.00530	-0.00175	-0.00951	0.0832
	(1.742)*	(1.242)	(-2.473)**	(-0.181)	
$Open_t$ - $Close_t$	-0.00030	-0.01305	0.00150	0.02574	0.0543
	(-0.220)	(-2.246)**	(1.554)	(0.391)	
Iron & Steel					
$Close_{t-1}$ - $Close_t$	-0.00031	0.01069	0.00087	-0.00333	0.0146
	(-0.115)	(-0.966)	(0.470)	(-0.029)	
$Close_{t-1}$ - $Open_t$	0.00146	-0.02061	0.00301	0.00486	0.0209
	(0.404)	(-1.393)	(1.220)	(0.036)	
$Open_t$ - $Close_t$	-0.00156	0.00867	0.00184	-0.00690	0.0134
	(-0.639)	(0.868)	(-1.104)	(-0.037)	
EWMKTR					
$Close_{t-1}$ - $Close_t$	-0.00072	-0.00496	0.00016	-0.00360	0.0026
	(-0.266)	(-1.517)	(0.568)	(-1.105)	

Note: t statistics in parentheses; ** (*) denotes significance at the 5 (10) percent level.

Table 5.15

U.S. Monthly Trade Deficit Announcement Effects On NT$/US$ Exchange Rate and Taiwanese Export-Oriented Firms' Stock Prices For Two Subperiods

OLS:	$R_{it} = a_i + b_i NEWS_t + e_{it}$

i=Individual Portfolio.

t=Announcement date.

News=Trade deficit forecast error as a percentage of expected trade deficit.

R=Daily exchange rate change or stock return.

Panel A: (49 obs. from Feb. 1980 to April 1984)

R_{it}	Constant	News	R^2	# of Firms
Exchange Rate Change				
$Close_{t-1}$ - $Close_t$	-0.00120	0.00584	0.0128	
	(-0.282)	(0.780)		
Electric & Machinary				3
$Close_{t-1}$ - $Close_t$	0.00969	0.00261	0.0209	
	(6.531)**	(1.001)		
$Close_{t-1}$ - $Open_t$	-0.00083	-0.00180	0.0339	
	(-1.047)	(-1.284)		
$Open_t$ - $Close_t$	0.00925	0.00232	0.0177	
	(6.432)**	(0.921)		
Electric Products				7
$Close_{t-1}$ - $Close_t$	0.00072	-0.00761	0.1031	
	(0.384)	(-2.325)**		
$Close_{t-1}$ - $Open_t$	-0.00014	-0.00133	0.0221	
	(-0.187)	(-1.030)		
$Open_t$ - $Close_t$	0.00065	-0.00683	0.1103	
	(0.403)	(-2.414)**		
Iron & Steel				1
$Close_{t-1}$ - $Close_t$	0.00055	-0.00523	0.0164	
	(0.161)	(-0.886)		
$Close_{t-1}$ - $Open_t$	0.00238	-0.00686	0.0302	
	(0.738)	(-1.210)		
$Open_t$ - $Close_t$	-0.00187	0.00159	0.0117	
	(-1.536)	(0.747)		
EWMKTR				
$Close_{t-1}$ - $Close_t$	-0.00037	-0.00386	0.0412	
	(-0.239)	(-1.421)		

Table 5.15 (continued)

Panel B: (49 obs. from May. 1984 to . 1988)

R_{it}	Constant	News	R^2	# of Firms
Exchange Rate Change				
$Close_{t-1} - Close_t$	-0.01234	-0.00708	0.0035	
	(-4.031)**	(-0.398)		
Electric & Machinary				3
$Close_{t-1} - Close_t$	0.01399	-0.00348	0.0024	
	(7.802)**	(-0.333)		
$Close_{t-1} - Open_t$	0.00226	-0.02398	0.0936	
	(1.211)	(-2.204)**		
$Open_t - Close_t$	0.01117	-0.00215	0.0008	
	(5.977)**	(-0.198)		
Electric Products				7
$Close_{t-1} - Close_t$	0.00216	-0.01483	0.0220	
	(0.874)	(-1.029)		
$Close_{t-1} - Open_t$	0.00227	-0.02406	0.1064	
	(1.301)	(-2.366)**		
$Open_t - Close_t$	-0.00005	0.00920	0.0121	
	(-0.022)	(0.760)		
Iron & Steel				1
$Close_{t-1} - Close_t$	-0.00007	-0.01987	0.0190	
	(-0.019)	(-0.912)		
$Close_{t-1} - Open_t$	0.00315	-0.01511	0.0042	
	(0.508)	(0.427)		
$Open_t - Close_t$	-0.00254	0.03001	0.0302	
	(-0.560)	(-1.158)		
EWMKTR				
$Close_{t-1} - Close_t$	0.00160	-0.01103	0.0146	
	(0.706)	(-0.835)		

Note: t statistics in parentheses; ** (*) denotes significance at the 5 (10) percent level.

period, which is consistent with the assertion that market participants paid more attention to the trade deficit news in the second subperiod. Also in the second subperiod the response to the trade deficit news was concentrated in overnight returns which suggests the trade deficit news is more quickly incorporated into stock prices.

5.5 Summary and Comments

In general, the results in this chapter support the protection hypothesis. The strong protectionist sentiment in the U.S. which was caused by large trade deficits and which may have led to trade restrictions did have a negative impact on stock prices of Taiwanese export-oriented firms. However, the trade news effect was different across industries and across firms. It is interesting to note that the trade conflict news effect was mainly reflected in the steel industry, while the trade deficit news effect was reflected in the electric machinery & machinery industry and the electronic industry. They seem to complement each other. This may also suggest that different industries are sensitive to different kinds of trade news. For trade deficit news, the effect was time-varying and it was the strongest in the second subperiod. For trade conflict events, many of them might have been anticipated before the press date.

Notes

[1] The data used in this paragraph are taken from Kuo (1978), Kuo and Fei (1985) and *Foreign Trade Statistics*, (1989) Department of Commerce, .

[2] It is well known in econometrics that for a regression of more than a thousand observations, the estimated coefficients have a higher chance to be statistically significant. The usual solution to this problem is to use the 5 or even 1 percent level of significance as the cutoff point.

VI

Empirical Investigation for South Korea Export-Oriented Firms

6.1 Background

After recovering from the war in the 1950s, the growth of South Korea's economy accelerated. Its GDP grew at an average of 9.5 percent per annum in the 1960s and 9 percent per annum in the 1970s. During this period South Korea transformed itself from an agricultural economy into a newly industrialized country. Although the growth rate slowed down in the 1980s, its performance was still relatively good compared with many other countries. Like Taiwan, the Korean economy can be characterized as an export-oriented economy. Its fast growth has relied heavily on exports, and for most of the 1970s and 1980s, the U.S. was the largest market for Korean export manufacturers. In the 1980s, Korea ran a large bilateral trade surplus with the U.S. and in the second half of the 1980s this surplus was ranked fifth among all U.S. trading partners.

The large trade surplus caused conflicts between the U.S. and Korea. Similar to Taiwan, South Korea was frequently named by the U.S. as an unfair trading partner in the 1980s, especially in the second half of the 1980s. The U.S. kept pressing Korea to open its domestic markets, decontrol its exchange rate, and self-restrain its exports to the U.S. Reluctantly, Korea bent toward this pressure from time to time to head off the possible U.S. trade restrictions against its exports. Considering the importance of U.S. markets to Korean export-oriented firms, the trade conflict events and the U.S. trade deficit news should have some impact on their stock prices.

6.2 General U.S - Korea Trade Conflict News Effect

6.2.1 Event Description

14 general U.S - Korea trade conflict events were identified from the *WSJ* during the period from 1984 to 1988. The first event was made public on March 9, 1984 and the last on May 9, 1988. Table 6.1 lists these events, their press dates, and each event's expected impact on the export-oriented firms' stock prices.

6.2.2 Data of Korean Export-Oriented Firms

The export-oriented firms were identified according to industries. A review of the *USITC Annual Report* in the 1980s reveals that five Korean industries were often caught in trade conflicts between the U.S. and Korea. They were apparel, rubber & tire, electronic & electric, motor vehicle, and iron & steel. Table 6.2 lists the five industries and the number of firms in each industry. However, at the end of 1984, Korea agreed to limit its annual shipments of finished steel to 1.9% of the U.S. market, thus the general trade conflicts, most of them happening after 1984, should not have much impact on the iron & steel industry. Therefore, we will focus on the other four industries. The firms in these industries with daily ($close_{t-1}$ to $close_t$) returns available on the PACAP data tape are selected as export-oriented firms.

The event day, day 0 and the day before the event day, day -1 are defined as before. Since Seoul time is 14 hours ahead of New York time (see figure 5.1), day -1 and day 0 are adjusted correspondingly. The sample period runs from 200 days prior to the first event (March 3, 1984) to 20 days after the last event (May 9, 1988).

6.2.3 Measuring Trade Conflict News Effects

Again we use the system of seemingly unrelated equations (3.24)

$$R_{jt} = \alpha_j + \beta_{j1}R_{mt-2} + \beta_{j2}R_{mt-1} + \beta_{j3}R_{mt} + \beta_{j4}R_{mt+1} + \beta_{j5}R_{mt+2} + \sum_{k=1}^{k} \gamma_{jk}D_{kt} + \varepsilon_{jk}$$

Table 6.1

Event Descriptions

This table lists 14 U.S-Korea trade conflict news items which may have had some general impact on Korean export-oriented industries during the mid-1980s

Event	Date	Descriptions
1	84/03/09	U.S. pressed Seoul to lower trade curbs as South Korea prepared export push.
		The predicted impact of this event on export-oriented firms' stock prices is ambiguous. If South Korea was expected to lower trade curbs, the impact might have been positive because it would ease the tension between the two countries; if not, the impact might have been negative since the export-oriented firms would face possible retaliations.
2	84/03/28	The Reagan administration announced major reductions in the duty-free privileges of Taiwan, Mexico, South Korea, and other third world countries.
		This event is predicted to have had a negative impact on the export-oriented firms because their products would lose some price competitiveness in U.S. markets.
	85/08/28	The Economic Policy Council recommended that President Reagan bring formal complaints against five trade practices of major U.S. trading partners, including Japan, South Korea, Brazil and a particular European subsidy.
		This event is predicted to have had a negative impact on the export-oriented firms because it raised the probability of U.S. trade restrictions.

Table 6.1 (Continued)

Event	Date	Descriptions
4	85/10/21	South Korea agreed to immediately open 10 industries to foreign investments and set a timetable for lifting import controls on 603 products over the next three years; the package was offered to the U.S. in response to strong U.S. pressure on South Korea.
		This event is predicted to have had a positive impact on export-oriented firms because it would ease the tension between the two countries.
5	85/11/07	The U.S. and South Korea were trading charges over Seoul's large trade surplus; the U.S. was losing patience with what it saw as South Korea's slow pace in opening home markets; Korean officials, meanwhile, were bristling at the U.S.'s unfair-trade actions against Seoul.
		This event is predicted to have had a negative impact on export-oriented firms because it increased the tension.
6	86/07/22	The Reagan administration announced that it won important trade concessions from South Korea, which it had accused of unfair trading practices; South Korea agreed to strengthen protection of foreign patents, trademarks and copyrights; separately, South Korea would permit South Korea citizens to purchase foreign made cigarettes.
		This event is predicted to have had a positive impact on export-oriented firms because it eased tensions.

Table 6.1 (Continued)

Event	Date	Descriptions
7	86/07/28	The Reagan administration was planning exchange-rate negotiations with Taiwan and South Korea in an effort to win a better break on trade; the move was ordered by Treasury Secretary James Baker, in response to mounting protectionist pressure. This event is predicted to have had a negative impact on export-oriented firms because it would reduce the price competitiveness of Korean firms in U.S. markets.
8	86/12/29	The South Korea government concerned about possible protectionist retaliation, planned to hold its 1987 trade surplus with the U.S. to the 1986 level by increasing imports from that country. This event is predicted to have had a positive impact on export-oriented firms because it might thwart some possible retaliations.
9	87/03/11	South Korea rejected the latest plea from Washington that it speed up the appreciation of its currency against the dollar to help reduce its mounting trade surplus with the U.S. The effect of this event is ambiguous because on the one hand it would keep the price competitiveness of export-oriented firms, on the other hand it might cause U.S. retaliations.

Table 6.1 (Continued)

Event	Date	Descriptions
10	87/04/07	South Korea, seeking to head off further trade frictions with the U.S., would cut tariff an average 6.6 percentage points, on imports of 83 manufactured and agricultural products; cuts would take effect July 1.
		This event is predicted to have had a positive impact on export-oriented firms because it would ease tensions.
11	88/02/01	The White House stripped certain trade benefits from four Asian countries with hopes they would decontrol their currency exchange rates; the move would make South Korea, Taiwan, Hong Kong, and Singapore ineligible as of 1989 for tariff-free treatment of some imports under the Generalized System of Preferences.
		This event is predicted to have had a negative impact on the export-oriented firms because they would lose some trade benefits.
12	88/02/04	Taiwan and Korea, seeking to ease frictions with the U.S. and other trading partners, planned fresh measures to curb their surplus.
		The impact of this event is ambiguous since the fresh measures may include both import liberalizations and voluntary export restrictions.
13	88/02/17	U.S. trade representative Clayton Yeutter opened a probe of South Korea's cigarette import restriction and warned that curbs might lead to U.S. retaliation.

Table 6.1 (Continued)

Event	Date	Descriptions
		This event is predicted to have had a negative impact on the export-oriented firms because it increased the probability of raising protection against these firms.
14	88/05//09	South Korea would cut prices of import cigarettes by nearly 50% and lift import bans on four agricultural products to avoid trade retaliation from the U.S.
		This event is predicted to have had a positive impact on the export-oriented firms because it might thwart some pending U.S. retaliation.

Table 6.2
Korean Export-Oriented Industries and Firm Numbers

Industry	Number of Firms
Apparel	
Rubber & Tire	7
Electronic & Electric	19
Motor Vehicle	6
Iron & Steel	9

to measure the trade conflict news effect on Korean export-oriented firms' stock returns. The firms are grouped into four portfolios according to the industry. The portfolio returns are the simple average of firm returns in the portfolio. This time $j = 1,2,3$, and 4, one for each portfolio. 14 dummy variables, $K = 14$, in each equation are used to capture the effects of the 14 events respectively. The dummy equals 1 during the corresponding two-day or one-day event period and 0 otherwise. 1382 observations from 200 days prior to the first event to 20 days after the last event are used to estimate the SUR system (3.24).

The same two joint hypotheses,

$$H_0^1 : \sum_{j=1}^{3} \gamma_{jk} = 0$$

and

$$H_0^2 : \gamma_{jk} = 0 \quad \forall j$$

are tested and the 5 percent significance level is used as the cutoff point.

6.2.4 Results

Table 6.3 and 6.4 present the results of the SUR analysis for the two-day event period. Table 6.3 shows the two-day average abnormal returns and t-statistics for each of the 14 events across the four industry portfolios. Events 1, 2, 4, 9, and 10 produced statistically significant abnormal returns for some portfolios but other events did not produce statistically significant abnormal returns for any portfolio. Event 1 (U.S. pressed Seoul to lower trade curbs) and event 2 (The Reagan administration announced major reductions in the duty-free privileges of Taiwan, Mexico, and South Korea) produced abnormal returns only for the electronic & electric portfolio. For event 1, the abnormal return was positive 5.8 percent, and for event 2, 5.3 percent. Both are significant at the 1 percent level (t = 3.365 and 3.051 respectively). Event 4 (Korea agreed to immediately open 10 industries to foreign investments, etc.) and event 9 (South Korea rejected the latest U.S. plea that it should speed up the appreciation of its currency against the dollar to help reduce its surplus with the U.S.) produced statistically significant abnormal returns for the rubber & tire portfolio but not for the others. The abnormal return for event 4 was positive 4.4 percent, which is significant at the 5 percent level (t = 2.019) and positive 5.6 percent for event 9, which is significant at the 1 percent level (t = 2.576). Event 10 (South Korea would cut tariff to head off further U.S. trade restriction against its exports) produced significant impacts on the apparel portfolio and the car portfolio. The two-day average abnormal return was 11.8 percent for the apparel portfolio and 5.1 percent for the car portfolio. It is significant at the 1 percent level (t = 3.097) for the apparel and 5 percent (t = 2.039) for the car. The positive abnormal returns associated with events 1, 4, 9, and 10 are not inconsistent with our predictions (see Table 6.1), but for event 2 the positive abnormal return is inconsistent with our prediction.

As depicted in Table 6.4, the second null hypothesis which states that the event has no impact on any of the four portfolios is rejected only for events 1, 2 and 10. For events 1 and 10, the hypothesis is rejected at the 1 percent level (F = 3.2332 and 3.6513 respectively). For event 2, it is rejected at the 5 percent level (F = 2.6821). The first hypothesis that the event has no impact on the export-oriented firms as a whole can be rejected only for event 10 at the 1 percent level (F = 7.4898). This suggests that events 1 and 2 produced an impact on some of the portfolios but not on the export-oriented firms as a whole, while event 10 produced an impact not only on some of the portfolios but also on the export-oriented firms as a whole. For events 4 and 9, the impact is no longer significant.

Tables 6.5, 6.6 and 6.7 present the estimates of one-day abnormal returns for day -1 and day 0. Table 6.5 and 6.6 report the one-day abnormal returns and t-statistics for day -1 and day 0 respectively. Table 6.7 reports the F-statistics of the two joint hypothesis tests for day -1 and day 0 abnormal returns. On day -1, events 1 and 2 still produced positive abnormal returns on the electronic & electrical portfolio but the significance is reduced to 5 percent. Event 10 produced positive abnormal return for the apparel but not for the car portfolio and the significance is also reduced to 5 percent level for the apparel. Events 4 and 9 did not produce any abnormal return on day -1. On day 0, only events 1 and 10 produced significant abnormal returns on the electronic & electrical portfolio and the apparel portfolio respectively, and both have significance at 5

Table 6.3

Korean Export-Oriented Industries' Abnormal Returns Around the Information Release of the Trade Conflict Between the U.S. and Korea, Averaged over Days -1 through 0, Where Day 0 Is the *WSJ* Announcement Date.

SUR:

$$R_{it} = \beta_{i0} + \beta_{i1} R_{mt-2} + \beta_{i2} R_{mt-1} + \beta_{i3} R_{mt} + \beta_{i4} R_{mt+1} + \beta_{i5} R_{mt+2} +$$

$$\sum_{k=1}^{k} a_{ik} D_{kt} + e_{it}$$

i = Individual Industry

t = 200 days prior to the first event to 20 days after the last event, altogether 1382 observations.

K = 14, there are 14 events.

Event	Apparel n=6	Rubber & Tire n=7	Electronic & Electrical n=19	Car n=6
Dum1	-0.02360	-0.02901	0.05819	0.01892
	(-0.626)	(-1.325)	(3.365)**	(0.767)
Dum2	-0.01786	-0.01800	0.05276	0.02564
	(-0.473)	(-0.822)	(3.051)**	(1.039)
Dum3	-0.01645	-0.02421	0.00348	-0.02166
	(-0.436)	(-1.106)	(0.201)	(-0.878)
Dum4	-0.02477	0.04423	-0.00939	-0.02794
	(-0.657)	(2.019)*	(-0.543)	(-1.132)
Dum5	-0.01361	-0.00364	-0.01023	0.04719
	(-0.361)	(-0.166)	(-0.591)	(1.913)
Dum6	0.00374	0.00607	-0.00887	-0.00114
	(0.099)	(0.277)	(-0.512)	(-0.046)
Dum7	-0.02748	-0.00474	0.01116	-0.01156
	(-0.729)	(-0.217)	(0.646)	(-0.469)

Table 6.3 (Continued)

Event	Apparel n=6	Rubber & Tire n=7	Electronic & Electrical n=19	Car n=6
Dum8	0.00933	0.00158	-0.00138	0.02282
	(0.246)	(0.072)	(-0.079)	(0.918)
Dum9	0.00185	0.05646	-0.02539	-0.03402
	(0.049)	(2.576)**	(-1.467)	(-1.378)
Dum10	0.11769	-0.01252	-0.01672	0.05068
	(3.097)**	(-0.567)	(-0.960)	(2.039)*
Dum11	-0.03573	-0.01363	0.00968	-0.02565
	(-0.945)	(-0.621)	(0.558)	(-1.037)
Dum12	-0.02281	-0.01362	-0.00114	-0.03119
	(-0.604)	(-0.621)	(-0.066)	(-1.262)
Dum13	-0.00573	-0.00995	0.01523	-0.00044
	(-0.152)	(-0.454)	(0.880)	(-0.018)
Dum14	-0.22683	-0.01317	0.02050	0.00425
	(-0.601)	(-0.601)	(1.186)	(0.172)

Note: t statistics in parentheses. ** (*) denotes significance at 1 (5) percent.

Table 6.4

Hypothesis Tests For Korean Export-Oriented Industries During Day -1 And Day 0

Event	$H_0^1: \sum_{l=1}^{3} a_{lk} = 0$ F(1, 5364)	$H_0^2: a_{lk} = 0 \quad \forall_l$ F(4, 5364)
Dum1	0.2357	3.2332**
Dum2	0.7105	2.6821*
Dum3	1.3604	0.6614
Dum4	0.1253	1.3468
Dum5	0.1525	1.0377
Dum6	0.0000	0.0798
Dum7	0.4180	0.2916
Dum8	0.4051	0.2429
Dum9	0.0005	2.2456
Dum10	7.4898**	3.6513**
Dum11	1.6683	0.6969
Dum12	1.8493	0.6903
Dum13	0.0003	0.2319
Dum14	0.0484	0.4827

Note: ** (*) denotes significance at 1 (5) percent.

percent. Comparing with the two-day results, we find that the two-day event period return captured more trade conflict effects than either the return for day -1 or day 0. This is further confirmed by comparing the results shown in Table 6.7 with that shown in Table 6.4. On day -1 none of the null joint hypotheses can be rejected, and on day 0 only the first hypothesis for event 10 can be rejected at the 5 percent level. It is much weaker than that shown in Table 6.4.

Considering the possibility that some of the events in Table 6.1 might have been anticipated or known by the market participants before the press date, the results here lend some support to our general hypothesis that the trade conflict news has had some impact on the export-oriented firms.

6.3 Specific U.S - Korea Trade Conflict News Effect

Five news items concerning dumping cases against Korean color-TV set exports during the period 1983-1985 are identified from the *WSJ* as specific U.S-Korea trade conflict events. Table 6.8 lists these events, their press dates, and the predicted impacts on the Korean color-TV set producers.

The daily (close$_{t-1}$ to close$_t$) stock returns of two major Korean color-TV set producers in this period are obtained from the PACAP data tape. They are Goldstar and Samsung. 677 observations from 200 days prior to the first event to 20 days after the last event are used to estimate the SUR system (20). There are two equations, one for each firm, in the system. There are five dummy variables in each equation for the five events in the dumping case. The two-day event period (day -1 and day 0) is defined as before and the same two joint hypotheses are tested.

Table 6.9 presents the results of the SUR analysis for the two-day event period. Panel A lists the two-day average abnormal returns for the five event periods across the two firms and their corresponding t-statistics. Event 4 (the ITC ruled that imports of color-TV sets from South Korea and Taiwan were injuring domestic producers) produced a two-day average abnormal return of -2.2 percent for Goldstar and -1.7 for Samsung. It is significant at 5 percent (t = -2.444) for Goldstar and 10 percent (t = -1.737) for Samsung. The strong negative responses of the two firms' stock prices are consistent with the prediction. The final ITC ruling that domestic firms were injured

Table 6.5

Korean Export-Oriented Industries' Abnormal Returns on Day -1, the Day Before the Trade Conflict News Appeared in the *WSJ*.

SUR:

$$R_{it} = \beta_{i0} + \beta_{i1}R_{mt-2} + \beta_{i2}R_{mt-1} + \beta_{i3}R_{mt} + \beta_{i4}R_{mt+1} + \beta_{i5}R_{mt+2} +$$

$$\sum_{k=1}^{k} a_{ik}D_{kt} + e_{it}$$

i = Individual Industry

t = 200 days prior to the first event to 20 days after the last event, altogether 1382 observations.

K = 14, there are 14 events.

Event	Apparel n=6	Rubber & Tire n=7	Electronic & Electrical n=19	Car n=6
Dum1	-0.01898	-0.02480	0.05741	0.00631
	(-0.355)	(-0.798)	(2.337)*	(0.180)
Dum2	-0.01579	-0.01724	0.05997	0.02894
	(-0.295)	(-0.554)	(2.439)*	(0.826)
Dum3	-0.01182	-0.02047	0.00558	-0.01809
	(-0.221)	(-0.659)	(0.227)	(-0.517)
Dum4	-0.04016	0.03275	-0.00863	-0.00963
	(-0.751)	(1.054)	(-0.351)	(-0.275)
Dum5	-0.01122	0.00119	-0.00759	0.05641
	(-0.210)	(0.038)	(-0.309)	(1.612)
Dum6	0.02568	0.00544	-0.01589	-0.00586
	(0.480)	(0.175)	(-0.647)	(-0.167)
Dum7	-0.02573	-0.01160	-0.00018	-0.02212
	(-0.481)	(-0.373)	(-0.008)	(-0.632)
Dum8	0.01607	-0.00654	0.01212	0.01735
	(0.300)	(-0.210)	(0.492)	(0.494)

Table 6.5 (Continued)

Event	Apparel n=6	Rubber & Tire n=7	Electronic & Electrical n=19	Car n=6
Dum9	-0.00483	0.05408	-0.01021	-0.02733
	(-0.090)	(1.740)	(-0.416)	(-0.781)
Dum10	0.12069	-0.01551	-0.02305	0.05279
	(2.245)*	(-0.496)	(-0.933)	(1.500)
Dum11	-0.02757	-0.00841	0.01302	-0.01686
	(-0.515)	(-0.270)	(0.529)	(-0.481)
Dum12	-0.02468	-0.00942	0.00971	-0.03001
	(-0.461)	(-0.209)	(0.395)	(-0.856)
Dum13	-0.01654	-0.01303	0.01845	0.00539
	(-0.309)	(-0.419)	(0.751)	(0.154)
Dum14	-0.02379	-0.00769	0.02373	0.03497
	(-0.445)	(-0.248)	(0.967)	(0.003)

Note: t statistics in parentheses. ** (*) denotes significance at 1 (5) percent.

Table 6.6

Korean Export-Oriented Industries' Abnormal Returns on Day 0, the Day the Trade Conflict News Appeared in the *WSJ*.

SUR:

$$R_{it} = \beta_{i0} + \beta_{i1} R_{mt-2} + \beta_{i2} R_{mt-1} + \beta_{i3} R_{mt} + \beta_{i4} R_{mt+1} + \beta_{i5} R_{mt+2} + \sum_{k=1}^{k} a_{ik} D_{kt} + e_{it}$$

i = Individual Industry

t = 200 days prior to the first event to 20 days after the last event, altogether 1382 observations.

K = 14, there are 14 events.

Event	Apparel n=6	Rubber & Tire n=7	Electronic & Electrical n=19	Car n=6
Dum1	-0.02505	-0.03321	0.05878	0.03154
	(-0.525)	(-1.071)	(2.393)*	(0.902)
Dum2	-0.02001	-0.01863	0.04540	0.02229
	(-0.374)	(-0.600)	(1.847)	(0.637)
Dum3	-0.02099	-0.02791	0.00129	-0.02526
	(-0.393)	(-0.900)	(0.053)	(-0.722)
Dum4	-0.00918	0.05573	-0.01025	-0.04623
	(-0.172)	(1.796)	(-0.417)	(-1.322)
Dum5	-0.01577	-0.00848	-0.01295	0.03798
	(-0.295)	(-0.273)	(-0.528)	(1.087)
Dum6	-0.01773	0.00662	-0.00196	0.00366
	(-0.331)	(0.213)	(-0.080)	(0.104)
Dum7	-0.02900	0.00211	0.02235	-0.00095
	(-0.543)	(0.068)	(0.910)	(-0.027)
Dum8	0.00372	-0.00934	-0.01514	0.02849
	(0.069)	(-0.300)	(0.614)	(0.811)

Table 6.6 (Continued)

Event	Apparel n=6	Rubber & Tire n=7	Electronic & Electrical n=19	Car n=6
Dum9	0.00890	0.05881	-0.04073	-0.04067
	(0.166)	(1.895)	(-1.657)	(-1.164)
Dum10	0.11417	-0.00921	-0.01064	0.04832
	(2.123)*	(-0.295)	(-0.431)	(1.373)
Dum11	-0.04403	-0.01868	0.00606	-0.03458
	(-0.821)	(-0.600)	(0.246)	(-0.986)
Dum12	-0.02038	-0.01791	-0.01211	-0.03232
	(-0.380)	(-0.576)	(-0.492)	(-0.922)
Dum13	0.00517	-0.00682	0.01187	-0.00625
	(0.097)	(-0.220)	(0.483)	(-0.179)
Dum14	-0.02140	-0.01863	0.01717	0.00838
	(-0.400)	(-0.601)	(0.699)	(0.240)

Note: t statistics in parentheses. ** (*) denotes significance at 1 (5) percent.

Table 6.7
Hypothesis Tests For Korean Export-Oriented Industries

$$H_0^1: \sum_{l=1}^{3} a_{lk} = 0 \qquad\qquad H_0^2: a_{lk} = 0 \quad \forall_l$$

Panel A: For Day -1

Event	F(1, 5364)	F(4, 5364)
Dum1	0.0777	1.4610
Dum2	0.6087	1.6900
Dum3	0.3919	0.2331
Dum4	0.1287	0.4686
Dum5	0.2941	0.7182
Dum6	0.0171	0.1644
Dum7	0.6948	0.2196
Dum8	0.2949	0.1509
Dum9	0.0268	0.8285
Dum10	3.5141	2.0318
Dum11	0.3084	0.2081
Dum12	0.5761	0.3152
Dum13	0.0064	0.1896
Dum14	0.0114	0.2785

Panel B: For Day 0

Dum1	0.1653	1.7997
Dum2	0.1650	1.0068
Dum3	1.0389	0.4489
Dum4	0.0193	1.0782
Dum5	0.0001	0.3852
Dum6	0.0173	0.0489
Dum7	0.0059	0.2801
Dum8	0.1352	0.2987
Dum9	0.0367	1.6205
Dum10	3,9342*	1.7904
Dum11	1.6177	0.5643
Dum12	1.3315	0.4887
Dum13	0.0031	0.0813
Dum14	0.0411	0.2274

Note: ** denotes significance at 5 percent; * denotes significance at 1 percent.

Table 6.8

Event Descriptions

This table lists 5 U.S. trade restriction events concerning imports of color-TV sets from South Korea and Taiwan between 1983-1985 and their expected impacts on Korean color-TV set producers.

Event	Date	Descriptions
1	83/06/10	The U.S. International Trade Commission ruled that imports of Color-TV sets from South Korea and Taiwan may be harming U.S. producers.
		This event is predicted to have had a negative impact on Korean color-TV firms since it increased the probability of imposing trade restrictions against these firms' exports to the U.S. markets.
2	83/10/13	U.S. Commerce Department ruled South Korea and Taiwan were exporting color-TV sets in the U.S. at unfairly low prices in violation of the anti-dumping act.
		This event is predicted to have had a negative impact on Korean color-TV set producers since it further increased the probability of imposing trade restrictions against these firms exports to the U.S. markets.
3	84/02/27	A government finding that some South Korea and Taiwanese firms were selling color-TV sets in the U.S. at below home market prices may lead to the imposition of anti-dumping duties.
		This event is predicted to have had a negative impact on Korean color-TV set producers since it further increased the probability of imposing trade restrictions against these firms exports to the U.S. markets.

Table 6.8 (continued)

Event	Date	Descriptions
4	84/04/06	The USITC ruled on April 5 that imports of color-TV sets from South Korea and Taiwan were injuring domestic producers.
		This event is predicted to have had a negative impact on Korean color-TV set producers since the anti-dumping duty on color-TV sets imported from Korea would be levied.
5	84/12/31	Three South Korea color-TV producers won substantial reductions in U.S. penalties because the companies submitted better documentation of manufacturing costs and home-market pricing.
		This event is predicted to have had positive impact on some Korean color-TV set producers.

would lead to anti-dumping duties to be levied against Korean and Taiwanese color-TV products, which consequently could have a negative impact on Korean color-TV producers. Event 5 (Korean TV producers had won substantial reductions in U.S. penalties because they submitted better documentation of manufacturing costs and home-market pricing) caused a positive 3 percent abnormal return during the two-day period and it is significant at 1 percent (t = 2.946). It is also consistent with the prediction. Panel B lists the F-statistics for the joint hypothesis tests. Both hypotheses can be rejected for events 4 and 5 at the 5 percent significance level. This indicates that both events had impact on some individual firms as well as the portfolio of all the firms.

Table 6.10 and 6.11 present the results for day -1 and day 0 separately. On day -1, event 3 (anti-dumping duties might be imposed on Korean and Taiwanese color-TV producers) had significant negative impact on both firms but other events did not. For Goldstar,

Table 6.9

Test Statistics for Korean TV-Set Export Firms' Abnormal Returns Averaged over Days -1 through 0, Where Day 0 Is the *WSJ* Announcement Date.

SUR:

$$R_{it} = \beta_{i0} + \beta_{i1}R_{mt-2} + \beta_{i2}R_{mt-1} + \beta_{i3}R_{mt} + \beta_{i4}R_{mt+1} + \beta_{i5}R_{mt+2} +$$

$$\sum_{k=1}^{k} a_{ik}D_{kt} + e_{it}$$

i = individual firm (1,2)

t = 200 days prior to the first event date to 20 days after the last event date, altogether 677 observations.

$K = 5$, there are 5 events.

Panel A

Event	Goldstar	Samsung
Dum1	-0.00242	-0.00577
	(-0.272)	(-0.594)
Dum2	0.00495	0.00604
	(0.556)	(0.622)
Dum3	-0.00920	-0.01049
	(-1.033)	(-1.080)
Dum4	-0.02169	-0.01681
	(-2.444)**	(-1.737)*
Dum5	0.00582	0.03015
	(0.620)	(2.946)**

Panel B

	Hypothesis Tests	
	$H_0^1 : \sum_{i=1}^{2} a_{ik} = 0$	$H_0^2 : a_{ik} = 0, \forall i$
Event	F(1, 1332)	F(2, 1332)
Dum1	0.2315	0.1908
Dum2	0.4165	0.2106
Dum3	1.3385	0.6699
Dum4	5.1531**	2.9949**
Dum5	4.0223**	6.0092**

Note: t statistics in parentheses in panel A; **(*) denotes significance at 5 (10) percent.

the abnormal return is -2.6 percent, which is significant at 5 percent
(t = -2.056). For Samsung, it is -2.5 percent, which is significant at
10 percent (t = -1.806). The joint hypothesis tests also show the
significance for event 3. The first hypothesis is significant at 5
percent, and the second is significant at 10 percent. On day 0, the
significant impact is associated with events 4 and 5. Event 4
produced -2.4 percent abnormal return for Goldstar, which is
significant at 10 percent (t = -1.906). Event 5 produced 4.3 percent
abnormal return for Samsung, which is significant at 5 percent (t =
3.025). For event 4, the first joint hypothesis can be rejected at the 10
percent significance level, and for event 5, both hypotheses can be
rejected at the 10 percent level. All the significant abnormal returns
found in Table 6.10 and 6.11 have the correct signs as predicted.

Comparing the results across tables 6.9-6.11, we find that events
1 and 2 had no impact on any firm at all. The reason for this might
be that these events only involved preliminary rulings which might be
subject to change later. Therefore, the investors might just wait and
see. The impact of event 3 is only captured on day -1, and the impact
of events 4 and 5 is captured on day 0 as well as the two-day event
period. It seems that the two-day event period dilutes the impact of
event 3. On the whole, the results in this section strongly support our
hypothesis that the U.S. trade restriction affects foreign export-
oriented firms.

6.4 U.S. Trade Deficit News Effect

Equation (3.30) (see Table 6.13) is used to examine the trade
deficit news effect on Korean export-oriented firms. The trade deficit
news data is the same as used in the previous chapters. The export-
oriented firms are grouped into five industry portfolios as listed in
Table 6.2. The daily (close$_{t-1}$ to close$_t$) and intradaily (close$_{t-1}$ to open$_t$
and open$_t$ to close$_t$) returns for the five industry portfolios and the
equally weighted market index (EWMKTR) around trade deficit
announcements, and the daily exchange rate change around the
announcements are used as dependent variables. For the whole
sample period (February, 1980 to December, 1988) the trade deficit
announcements came when the Seoul Stock Exchange was closed
(see figure 5.1). There are 99 observations during this period. The
portfolio return is the simple average of individual firm returns in the

Table 6.10

Test Statistics for Korean TV-Set Export Firms' Abnormal Returns on Day -1, the Day Before the News Appeared in the *WSJ*.

Panel A

SUR:

$$R_{it} = \beta_{i0} + \beta_{i1}R_{mt-2} + \beta_{i2}R_{mt-1} + \beta_{i3}R_{mt} + \beta_{i4}R_{mt+1} + \beta_{i5}R_{mt+2} +$$

$$\sum_{k=1}^{k} a_{ik}D_{kt} + e_{it}$$

i = individual firm (1,2)

t = 200 days prior to the first event date to 20 days after the last event date, altogether 677 observations.

K = 5, there are 5 events.

Event	Goldstar	Samsung
Dum1	-0.00907	-0.01257
	(-0.724)	(-0.915)
Dum2	0.00078	0.00357
	(0.062)	(0.259)
Dum3	-0.02583	-0.02486
	(-2.056)**	(-1.806)*
Dum4	-0.01938	-0.01665
	(-1.545)	(-1.211)
Dum5	0.00409	0.01515
	(0.317)	(1.072)

Panel B

	Hypothesis Tests	
	$H_0^1: \sum_{i=1}^{2} a_{ik} = 0$	$H_0^2: a_{ik} = 0, \forall i$
Event	F(1, 1332)	F(2, 1332)
Dum1	0.8123	0.4295
Dum2	0.0326	0.0448
Dum3	4.4391**	2,2809*
Dum4	2.2499	1.2221
Dum5	0.6073	0.7197

Note: t statistics in parentheses in panel A; ** denotes significance at 5 percent and * at 10 percent.

Table 6.11

Test Statistics for Korean TV-Set Export Firms' Abnormal Returns on Day 0, the Day the News Appeared in the *WSJ*.

Panel A

SUR:

$$R_{it} = \beta_{i0} + \beta_{i1} R_{mt-2} + \beta_{i2} R_{mt-1} + \beta_{i3} R_{mt} + \beta_{i4} R_{mt+1} + \beta_{i5} R_{mt+2} +$$

$$\sum_{k=1}^{k} a_{ik} D_{kt} + e_{it}$$

i = individual firm (1,2)

t = 200 days prior to the first event date to 20 days after the last event date, altogether 677 observations.

K = 5, there are 5 events.

Event	Goldstar	Samsung
Dum1	0.00442	0.00064
	(0.349)	(0.046)
Dum2	0.00912	0.00847
	(0.725)	(0.617)
Dum3	0.00769	0.00409
	(0.609)	(0.297)
Dum4	-0.02395	-0.01696
	(-1.906)*	(-1.238)
Dum5	0.00745	0.04297
	(0.572)	(3.025)**

Panel B

Hypothesis Tests

Event	$H_0^1: \sum_{i=1}^{2} a_{ik} = 0$	$H_0^2: a_{ik} = 0, \forall i$
	F(1, 1332)	F(2, 1332)
Dum1	0.0436	0.0932
Dum2	0.5343	0.2779
Dum3	0.2376	0.1967
Dum4	2.8989*	1.8173
Dum5	4.0980**	6.5274**

Note: t statistics in parentheses in panel A; ** denotes significance at 5 percent and * at 10 percent.

Table 6.12

Hypothesized Trade Deficit News Signals and the Expected Signs of Their Impacts on Stock Prices

Stock Return Response	Korean Export-Oriented Firms
Reducing U.S. Spending	-
Dollar Depreciation without Inflation	-
Dollar Depreciation with Inflation	+
Increasing U.S. Protection	-
Losing U.S Competitiveness	+

Note: + denotes positive impact; - negative.

portfolio. Based on our discussion in section 3.2.2, the hypothesized trade deficit news effects on the export-oriented firms are summarized in Table 6.12.

The trade deficit news effect on the market return is expected to be insignificant because of the "watering down" effect. If not, the effect would be the same as that on the export-oriented firms. The trade deficit news effect on Won/$ exchange rate is also expected to be insignificant since for most of the period under investigation, the Korean won was pegged to the US$. However, if trade deficit news had some impact on the won/$ exchange rate, then a larger than expected trade deficit should be associated with an appreciation of the Korean won because the U.S. often pressed Korea in the second half of the 1980s to appreciate its currency against the U.S. dollar hence to reduce its large trade surplus with the U.S. Although the Korean government still controlled the exchange rates, there was a tendency to decontrol in the late 1980s.

Table 6.13 presents the estimation results of equation (3.30) for the whole sample period. As expected, the trade deficit news had no impact on the exchange rate as well as the market return. However, two out of the five portfolios had significant responses to the trade deficit news. For the apparel portfolio the response occurred in the daily (close$_{t-1}$ to close$_t$) return and the estimated ß is 0.01640 which is significant at the 10 percent level (t = 1.662). For the iron & steel portfolio the response occurred in both the daily return and overnight (close$_{t-1}$ to open$_t$) return. The estimated ß for the daily return is -0.01334 which is significant at the 10 percent level (t = -1.895) and for the overnight return the ß is -0.00670 which is significant at the 5 percent level (t = -2.628).

Table 6.14 presents the estimation results of equation (3.32) the linearly time-varying trade deficit news effect hypothesis. The results for the apparel and rubber & tire portfolios support this hypothesis that the trade deficit news effect is linearly time-varying with the trade deficit level. For the apparel portfolio, the coefficient of the interactive term, NEWS*DEF, shows the 1 percent significance in both the daily return and trading time (open$_t$ to close$_t$) return. The estimated coefficients are 0.00795 (t = 2.944) and 0.00186 (t = 2.234) respectively. However, the computed means of the corresponding ß$_t$ is only significant for the daily return but not for the trading time return. For the daily return, ß$_t$ is 0.03751 which is significant at the 5 percent level (t = 2.299). For the rubber & tire portfolio, the estimated coefficient for the trading time return is 0.00166 which is significant at the 5 percent level (t = 1.852). The computed mean of ß$_t$ is 0.00919 which is significant at the 5 percent level (t = 1.955). This indicates the trade deficit news effect on apparel and rubber & tire portfolios is varying with the trade deficit level over time and on average the effect is positive and significant.

Table 6.15 presents the estimation results of equation (3.30) for the two subsample periods. Panel A shows the results for the first subperiod which is similar to the results of the whole sample period shown in Table 6.13. For the apparel daily return, ß = 0.1664 which is significant at the 10 percent level (t = 1.802), and for the iron & steel daily return, ß = -0.01663 which is also significant at the 10 percent level (t = -1.920). However, the overnight return for iron & steel showed no significant response to the trade deficit news, while in the whole sample period it showed a negative response which is significant at the 5 percent level. Panel B shows the results for the second subsample period. For the first time in the study the exchange rate showed a significant response to the trade deficit news. The news coefficient ß = -1.73574 which is significant at the 5 percent level. This indicates that a larger than expected trade deficit was associated with a won appreciation. For the apparel and electronic portfolios there was no response to the trade deficit news. For the rubber & tire and iron & steel portfolios the significant responses were found in the overnight return, and for the motor vehicle portfolio the significant response was found in the trading time return. For the rubber & tire, ß = 0.02913, which is significant at the 10 percent level (t = 1.794); for the iron & steel, ß = -0.01829, which is significant at the 5 percent level; and for the motor vehicle, ß = -0.62900, which is significant at the 10 percent level (t = 1.665).

The following inferences can be made from the above results. First, while there were significant industry portfolio responses to the trade deficit news in the whole sample period as well as in each of the two subsample periods, there was no significant response shown in the market return in any of these periods. This is consistent with our prediction that there exists a "watering down" effect in the market index. Second, the won/$ exchange rate showed no significant response to the trade deficit news in the whole sample period as well as the first subsample period but it did show a significant negative response to the trade deficit news in the second subsample period. This gives rise to the possibility that trade deficit news affected the export-oriented firms' stock prices in the second subsample period via exchange rate changes. Third, the trade deficit news effect was different across industries. In the whole sample period as well as the first subsample period, the trade deficit news effect was positive for the apparel portfolio which supports the hypothesis that the trade deficit news signals losing competitiveness of the corresponding U.S. firms. The effect was negative for the iron & steel portfolio which supports the protection hypothesis that the trade deficit news increased the probability of U.S. trade restrictions against Korean iron & steel firms. In the second subsample period, the trade deficit news effect was positive on the rubber & tire portfolio but negative on the iron & steel and motor vehicle portfolios. Since the exchange rate also had a significant negative response to the trade deficit news, it is hard to conclude that the negative portfolio response to the trade deficit news was due to an increased probability of raising U.S. trade protection or due to the appreciation of the won. However, the positive response of the rubber & tire portfolio is consistent with the losing competitiveness hypothesis since in a world with many competitive suppliers the appreciation of the won would not benefit Korean export-oriented firms. Also, the negative response of the steel portfolio in the second subsample period was probably caused by the appreciation of the won because Korea agreed to limit its annual shipment of finished steel to 1.9 percent of the U.S. market. Finally, the trade deficit news effect was changing over time. For the apparel and rubber & tire portfolios, the responses to the trade deficit news were linearly varying with the trade deficit level over time. For the apparel portfolio the response was significant in the first subsample period but not in the second. For the rubber & tire and motor vehicle portfolios, the responses were insignificant in the first subsample period but significant in the second subsample period. This supports the assertion that the trade deficit news effect is varying over time.

6.5 Summary and Comments

On the whole, the results in this chapter lend some support to our general hypothesis that U.S - Korea trade conflict events and the U.S. trade deficit news have had some impact on Korean export-oriented firms. For the specific trade conflict events, the response of Korean color-TV producers' stock prices are intuitive that U.S.-Korea trade conflict affect the Korean export-oriented firms. However, the evidence for trade conflict events is not very strong. Many general events had no impact on the export-oriented firms which may be due to the possibility that these events did not contain much information. For trade deficit news, the results seem to support both the protection hypothesis and the losing competitiveness hypothesis. The trade deficit news effect was different across industries and changed over time.

Table 6.13

U.S. Monthly Trade Deficit Announcement Effects On Won/Dollar Exchange Rate and Korean Export-Oriented Firms' Stock Prices.

OLS:	$R_{it} = a_i + b_i NEWS_t + e_{it}$

i=Individual Portfolio.

t=Annoucement date (from Feb. 1980 to Dec. 1988, altogether 99 observations).

News=Trade deficit forecast error as a percentage of expected trade deficit.

R=Daily exchange rate change or stock return.

R_{it}	Constant	News	R^2	# of Firms
Exchange Rate Change				
$Close_{t-1}$ - $Close_t$	0.12118	-0.17383	0.0116	
	(1.760)*	(-1.067)		
Apparel (79 obs.)				6
$Close_{t-1}$ - $Close_t$	0.01188	0.01640	0.0346	
	(3.054)**	(1.662)*		
$Close_{t-1}$ - $Open_t$	0.00109	0.00336	0.0071	
	(0.610)	(0.740)		
$Open_t$ - $Close_t$	0.00232	0.00342	0.0097	
	(0.867)	(1.157)		
Rubber & Tire				7
$Close_{t-1}$ - $Close_t$	0.01301	0.00737	0.0089	
	(3.888)**	(0.931)		
$Close_{t-1}$ - $Open_t$	0.00223	0.00457	0.0095	
	(1.110)	(0.964)		
$Open_t$ - $Close_t$	0.00108	0.00342	0.0136	
	(0.867)	(1.157)		

Table 6.13 (Continued)

R_{it}	Constant	News	R^2	# of Firm
Iron & Steel				9
$Close_{t-1} - Close_t$	0.01344	-0.01334	0.0357	
	(4.515)**	(-1.895)		
$Close_{t-1} - Open_t$	0.00150	-0.00670	0.0665	
	(1.391)	(-2.628)**		
$Open_t - Close_t$	0.00030	-0.00059	0.0008	
	(0.326)	(-0.273)		
Electronic Products				19
$Close_{t-1} - Close_t$	0.02035	-0.00226	0.0010	
	(6.774)**	(-0.313)		
$Close_{t-1} - Open_t$	0.00246	0.00116	0.0022	
	(2.298)**	(0.458)		
$Open_t - Close_t$	0.00581	-0.00745	0.0045	
	(1.219)	(-0.661)		
Motor Vehicle				6
$Close_{t-1} - Close_t$	0.02523	0.00204	0.0004	
	(5.613)**	(0.192)		
$Close_{t-1} - Open_t$	0.00067	0.00299	0.0057	
	(0.398)	(0.747)		
$Open_t - Close_t$	0.01685	-0.02964	0.0069	
	(1.105)	(-0.822)		
EWMKTR				
$Close_{t-1} - Close_t$	0.02033	-0.00297	0.0037	
	(9.728)**	(-0.601)		

Note: t statistics in parentheses; ** (*) denotes significance at 5 (10) percent.

Table 6..14

Linearly Time-Varying Trade News Effect On Korean Export-Oriented Firms' Stock Returns (98 observations from Feb. 1980 to Dec. 1988)

$$R_{it} = \alpha + c*NEWS_t + d*NEWS_tDEF_t + \varepsilon_{it}$$

Stock Return	Constant	NEWS	NEWS*DEF	dR/dNEWS	R^2
Apparel (79 obs.)					
$Close_{t-1}$ - $Close_t$	0.00892	-0.03078	0.00795	0.03751	0.1334
	(2.320)**	(-1.656)*	(2.944)**	(2.299)**	
$Close_{t-1}$ - $Open_t$	0.00079	-0.00139	0.00080	0.00548	0.0119
	(0.462)	(-0.155)	(0.612)	(0.693)	
$Open_t$ - $Close_t$	0.00162	-0.00846	0.00186	0.07517	0.0707
	(1.371)	(-1.477)	(2.234)**	(1.495)	
Rubber & Tire					
$Close_{t-1}$ - $Close_t$	0.01133	-0.01136	0.00367	0.02016	0.0321
	(3.234)**	(-0.776)	(1.517)	(1.592)	
$Close_{t-1}$ - $Open_t$	0.00194	0.00145	0.00061	0.00669	0.0113
	(0.916)	(0.164)	(0.417)	(0.873)	
$Open_t$ - $Close_t$	0.00032	0.00506	0.00166	0.00919	0.0476
	(0.247)	(-0.933)	(1.852)*	(1.955)**	
Iron & Steel					
$Close_{t-1}$ - $Close_t$	0.01237	-0.02523	0.00233	0.01749	0.0472
	(3.947)**	(-1.927)**	(1.077)	(1.544)	
$Close_{t-1}$ - $Open_t$	0.00189	-0.00238	-0.00084	-0.00968	0.0777
	(1.622)*	(-0.503)	(-1.079)	(-2.354)**	
$Open_t$ - $Close_t$	-0.00014	-0.00555	0.00097	0.00278	0.0227
	(-0.135)	(-1.385)	(1.467)	(0.802)	
Electronic Products					
$Close_{t-1}$ - $Close_t$	0.02142	0.00967	-0.00233	-0.01034	0.0127
	(6.769)**	(0.732)	(-1.067)	(-0.904)	
$Close_{t-1}$ - $Open_t$	0.00282	0.00519	-0.00079	-0.00160	0.0127
	(2.500)**	(1.099)	(-1.011)	(-0.391)	
$Open_t$ - $Close_t$	0.00731	0.00929	-0.00328	-0.01889	0.0137
	(1.455)	(0.443)	(-0.946)	(-1.040)	

Table 6.14 (Continued)

Stock Return	Constant	NEWS	NEWS*DEF	dR/dNEWS	R^2
Motor Vehicle					
$Close_{t-1}$ - $Close_t$	0.02504	-0.00012	0.00042	0.00349	0.0006
	(5.257)**	(-0.006)	(0.129)	(0.202)	
$Close_{t-1}$ - $Open_t$	0.00044	0.00039	0.00050	0.00469	0.0075
	(0.245)	(0.052)	(0.412)	(0.724)	
$Open_t$ - $Close_t$	0.02202	0.02796	-0.01128	-0.06893	0.0175
	(1.371)	(0.417)	(-1.018)	(-1.187)	
EWMKTR					
$Close_{t-1}$ - $Close_t$	0.02061	0.00019	-0.00062	-0.00514	0.0054
	(9.318)**	(0.021)	(-0.406)	(-0.643)	

Note: t statistics in parentheses; ** (*) denotes significance at 5 (10) percent.

Table 6.15

U.S. Monthly Trade Deficit Announcement Effects On Won/Dollar Exchange Rate and Korean Export-Oriented Firms' Stock Prices For Two Subperiods

OLS:	$R_{it} = a_i + b_i NEWS_t + e_{it}$			

i=Individual Portfolio.

t=Annoucement date.

News=Trade deficit forecast error as a percentage of expected trade deficit.

R=Daily exchange rate change or stockreturn.

Panel A: (47 obs. from Feb. 1980 to April 1984)

R_{it}	Constant	News	R^2	# of Firm
Exchange Rate Change				
$Close_{t-1}$ - $Close_t$	0.31692	-0.11565	0.0133	
	(3.719)**	(-0.788)		
Apparel (29 obs.)				6
$Close_{t-1}$ - $Close_t$	0.00522	0.01664	0.1074	
	(0.930)	(1.802)*		
$Close_{t-1}$ - $Open_t$	0.00077	0.00419	0.0189	
	(0.218)	(0.721)		
$Open_t$ - $Close_t$	0.00392	0.00056	0.0010	
	(1.861)	(0.162)		
Rubber & Tire				7
$Close_{t-1}$ - $Close_t$	0.00974	0.00599	0.0102	
	(1.889)*	(0.681)		
$Close_{t-1}$ - $Open_t$	-0.00016	0.00322	0.0109	
	(-0.062)	(0.705)		
$Open_t$ - $Close_t$	0.00237	0.00313	0.0132	
	(1.004)	(0.777)		
Iron & Steel				9
$Close_{t-1}$ - $Close_t$	0.01453	-0.01663	0.0757	
	(2.862)**	(-1.920)*		
$Close_{t-1}$ - $Open_t$	-0.00031	-0.00481	0.0492	
	(-0.168)	(-1.526)		
$Open_t$ - $Close_t$	0.00220	-0.00221	0.0156	
	(1.435)	(-0.845)		

Table 6.15 (continued)

R_{it}	Constant	News	R^2	# of Firms
Electronic Products				19
$Close_{t-1}$ - $Close_t$	0.02408	-0.00128	0.0005	
	(4.719)**	(-0.147)		
$Close_{t-1}$ - $Open_t$	0.00408	0.00053	0.0007	
	(2.280)**	(0.173)		
$Open_t$ - $Close_t$	0.00239	0.00103	0.0022	
	(1.233)	(0.313)		
Motor Vehicle				6
$Close_{t-1}$ - $Close_t$	0.02895	-0.00006	0.0000	
	(3.802)**	(-0.005)		
$Close_{t-1}$ - $Open_t$	0.00245	0.00091	0.0027	
	(1.595)	(0..346)		
$Open_t$ - $Close_t$	0.00087	-0.00026	0.0001	
	(0.367)	(-0.064)		
EWMKTR				
$Close_{t-1}$ - $Close_t$	0.02416	-0.00396	0.0080	
	(6.281)**	(-0.604)		

Panel B: (52 obs. from May. 1984 to Dec 1988)

Exchange Rate Change				
$Close_{t-1}$ - $Close_t$	-0.04991	-1.73574	0.1759	
	(-0.540)	(-3.234)**		
Apparel (50 obs.)				6
$Close_{t-1}$ - $Close_t$	0.01520	0.04201	0.0411	
	(2.965)**	(1..434)		
$Close_{t-1}$ - $Open_t$	0.00126	-0.00112	0.0002	
	(0.613)	(-0..096)		
$Open_t$ - $Close_t$	0.00151	0.01018	0.0322	
	(1.073)	(1..264)		

Table 6.15 (continued)

R_{it}	Constant	News	R^2	# of Firms
Rubber & Tire				7
$Close_{t-1} - Close_t$	0.01566	0.03616	0.0397	
	(3.595)**	(11.438)		
$Close_{t-1} - Open_t$	0.00414	0.02913	0.0576	
	(1..435)	(1.749)*		
$Open_t - Close_t$	0.00001	0.00069	0.0002	
	(0..009)	(0.106)		
Iron & Steel				9
$Close_{t-1} - Close_t$	0.01241	0.01595	0.0131	
	(3.651)**	(0.813)		
$Close_{t-1} - Open_t$	0.00307	-0.01829	0.1265	
	(2.604)**	(-2.691)**		
$Open_t - Close_t$	-0.00133	0.00781	0.0335	
	(-1.300)	(1.317)		
Electronic Products				19
$Close_{t-1} - Close_t$	0.01732	-0.02851	0.0404	
	(5.088)**	(-1.451)		
$Close_{t-1} - Open_t$	0.00111	0.00058	0.0001	
	(0.876)	(0.080)		
$Open_t - Close_t$	0.00897	-0.08029	0.0494	
	(1..039)	(-1.611)		
Motor Vehicle				6
$Close_{t-1} - Close_t$	0.02209	0.00744	0.0012	
	(4.186)**	(0..245)		
$Close_{t-1} - Open_t$	-0.00088	0.01671	0.0199	
	(-0.306)	(1.008)		
$Open_t - Close_t$	0.03122	-0.62900	0.0526	
	(1.116)	(-1.665)*		
EWMKTR				
$Close_{t-1} - Close_t$	0.01713	-0.00963	0.0141	
	(8.688)**	(-0.846)		

Note: t statistics in parentheses; ** (*) denotes significance at 5 (10) percent.

VII

Cross -Country Comparisons And Concluding Remarks

In view of all the empirical results in chapters 4, 5, and 6, we do find evidence that the trade deficit news and trade restrictions had an impact on US import-competing and Korean and Taiwanese export-oriented firms. The finding has the following patterns: first, the effect of the trade deficit news on stock prices of the trade related firms was more obvious than that of the trade restriction and trade conflict news; second, the specific trade conflict news and the U.S. trade deficit news produced a greater impact on Korean and Taiwanese export-oriented firms than on U.S. import-competing firms; third, for all three countries, the trade deficit news produced some impact on the corresponding import-competing firms and export-oriented firms but not on equally weighted market returns; fourth, the trade deficit news effect on U.S. firms lends some support for the losing competitiveness hypothesis but the trade deficit news effect on Korean and Taiwanese firms generally provides support for the protection hypothesis; and finally, the trade deficit news effect was more significant in the second half of the 1980s than in the first half. These results offer interesting contrasts to the results of earlier authors that focused solely on U.S. stock market prices. The availability of data for Taiwan and Korea allows for a greater understanding of the effects of U.S. trade restrictions than has been possible in the past.

In general, the trade related firms' stock prices were less sensitive to the trade restriction and trade conflict news than to the trade deficit news in all three countries. For U.S. firms, the "unfair trade practice" petitions and the subsequent decisions on these cases had no significant impact on the petitioners' stock prices from two days before to two days after. For Korean and Taiwanese export-oriented firms, although some trade conflict news events had significant impacts, most events did not. This pattern may due to the different qualities of the news identification. The trade deficit news is proxied in terms of the unexpected trade deficit as a share of the expected trade deficit and thus contains more information and involves more uncertainty. However, considering the routine legal and political processes for trade restriction and trade conflict events, the market participants may forecast many of these events, and thus when the news appeared in the Wall Street Journal, it might not have much information content to the market participants.

The U.S. trade deficit news significantly affected three out of eight U.S. import-competing industry portfolios only in the second subsample period and the significance was at the five percent level for only one portfolio. In contrast, the trade deficit news effect was significant in two out of three Taiwanese industry portfolios in both subsample periods as well as in the whole sample period. Most of the effects were significant at the five percent level. Korean firms also responded significantly to the trade deficit news in all sample periods: in two out of five industry portfolios in the whole sample period as well as in the first subsample period and three out of five in the second subsample period. The petitions filed with the ITC did not have any impact on the U.S. petition firms but did have a significant impact on Korean and Taiwanese color-TV firms. This pattern suggests that the U.S. trade deficit and trade restriction news had more impact on the export-oriented firms in the small open economy which heavily depended upon U.S. markets than on the import-competing firms at home, which is consistent with the prediction of the trade theory as discussed in Chapter 1.

Previous authors examined the trade deficit news effect on stock market indices. We argue that the effect may be watered down by non-trade related firms. The pattern we found in previous chapters (that none of the market returns in the three countries captured the trade deficit news effect) supports our argument. The fact that the Taiwanese market return did not reflect any trade deficit effect provides the strongest evidence for the "watering down" story. If the trade deficit news were to have any impact on market returns, it should have had an impact on the Taiwanese market return because the Taiwanese bilateral trade surplus with the U.S. was about 15 percent of the Taiwanese GNP during the second subsample period, which topped all major U.S. trading partners.

It seems strange that the pattern of the trade deficit news effect in the U.S. supports the losing competitiveness hypothesis, while in Taiwan and Korea it generally supports the protection hypothesis. However, it is perfectly plausible that the trade deficit news signalled trade restrictions to Korean and Taiwanese firms but losing competitiveness or not enough protection to the U.S. firms. This may occur because there were other competitors in the world and the trade restrictions are usually selective, i.e., country specific. This suggests that the possible U.S. trade restrictions would hurt Taiwan and Korea but benefit other countries.

For all three countries, the trade deficit news effect was more significant in the second subsample period than in the first. This is consistent with the assertion that the market participants paid more attention to the trade deficit news in the second subsample period than in the first. Also for Korean and Taiwanese export-oriented firms, it seems that the trade deficit news effect was more quickly incorporated in the second subsample period than in the first, i.e., during the second subsample period, more effects were captured in the overnight returns.

On the whole, our results support the hypothesis that the protection events and the trade deficit news have some impacts on the stock prices of import-competing firms and export-oriented firms in the relevant countries.

Appendices

A. "Unfair Trade" Petition Filing Firms, Petition Dates, And The ITC Final Decision Dates

	Complaint	Dateof Publication of Notice in Federal Register	Date Orders Issued	
1	Dennison Manufacturing Co.	77-08-11	80-03-20	-
2	Cyclotron Corp.	78-12-28	79-12-21	0
3	Vishay Interchange, Inc	79-01-17	80-05-09	0
4	Westinghouse Electric Corp.	79-03-28	81-07-07	0
5	High Voltage Engineering Corp.	79-06-27	80-12-29	+
6	Loctite Corp.	79-08-31	80-05-27	-
7	Stewart-Warner Corp.	79-12-19	81-06-19	+
8	PPG Industries, Inc.,	80-02-27	80-10-22	0
9	Talon Division of Textron, Inc.	80-06-11	81-01-12	-
10	Kuhlman Corp.	80-08-08	81-08-10	+
11	Dana Corp.	80-12-24	81-10-05	0
12	Western Marine Electronics, Inc.	81-06-10	82-06-09	-
13	Motorola, Inc.	81-03-11	82-04-13	0
14	The Scott & Fetzer Co.	81-12-23	82-10-01	0
15	Ideal Toy Corp.	81-12-29	82-12-30	+
16	Shopsmith, Inc.	82-01-28	82-12-28	0
17	Illinois Tool Works, Inc.	82-03-03	83-03-03	-
18	E.I. du Pont	82-04-21	83-04-21	+
19	Mattel, Inc.	82-12-29	83-06-29	0
20	Revere Copper & Brass, Inc.	83-03-16	83-09-19	0
21	Apple Computer Inc.	83-03-09	84-03-09	+
22	Textron Inc.	82-11-17	84-03-22	-
23	Clow Corp.	83-11-30	84-08-09	0
24	Outboard Marine Corp.	83-12-16	84-05-18	0
25	Minnesota Mining & Manufacturing Co.	83-06-08	84-05-24	+
26	Printronix, Inc.	83-07-27	84-03-14	0
27	Eldon Industries, Inc.	83-08-10	84-05-03	0
28	Masco Corp. of Indiana	83-10-24	84-10-24	+

	Complaint	Date of Publication	Date Orders issued
29	Union Carbide Corp.	83-10-26	84-11-26 +
30	Varian Associates Inc.	84-02-01	85-06-13 +
31	Cabot Corp.	84-02-29	85-03-04 +
32	Texas Instruments, Inc.	84-07-18	85-06-10 -
33	Baxter Travenol Laboratories, Inc.	84-10-11	85-04-01 0
34	Caterpillar Tractor Co.	84-12-05	85-04-03 0
35	Thomas & Betts Corp.	84-12-19	85-07-09 0
36	E.I. du Pont de Numours & Co.	84-05-23	85-11-25 +
37	Fisher & Porter Co.	85-10-30	86-10-30 -
38	Coleco Industries Inc.	85-11-07	86-11-07 +
39	Minnesota Mining & Manufacturing Co.	86-02-20	87-02-25 -
40	Texas Instruments	86-03-19	87-09-21 +
41	Pittway Corp.	6-11-13	87-06-29 0
42	Dataproducts Corp.	6-12-23	88-01-25 0
43	Supreme Equipment & Systems Corp.	7-03-19	87-12-07 0
44	Minnesota Mining & Manufacturing Co.	7-07-15	88-07-15 +
45	Motorola, Inc.	7-08-12	88-03-09 0
46	Dover Corp.	7-08-19	88-03-01 0
47	Intel Corp	87-09-16	89-03-16 +
48	Minnesota Mining & Manufacturing	89-03-22	89-08-16 0
49	Phillips Petroleum Co.	89-04-27	89-12-21 0
50	Motorola Inc.	89-05-31	89-12-29 0
51	Ingersoll-Rand Co.	90-05-03	91-06-18 -
52	Pall Corp.	91-01-16	91-03-27 0
53	Texas Instruments Inc.	90-08-15	92-02-18 +
54	Hologic, Inc.	91-02-27	91-12-03 0
55	Minnesota Mining & Manufacturing	91-12-26	92-05-06 0
56	Xoma Corp.	91-01-30	92-12-17 0
57	Modine Manufacturing Co.	92-01-23	93-06-25 -
58	The warner & Swasey	79-10-24	80-12-08 0

Note: the data are not available for cases 15 and 58 during the ruling period.

B. Trade Deficit Announcements and the Corresponding MMS
Forecasts

Month	Forecast	Survey Date	Actual	Release Date
1980				
January	-4.00	80-02-26	-4.80	80-02-28
February	-4.00	80-03-18	-5.60	80-03-27
March	-4.00	80-04-22	-3.20	80-04-29
April	-3.00	80-05-20	-1.90	80-05-28
May	-2.00	80-06-24	-4.00	80-06-27
June	-2.50	80-07-22	-2.30	80-07-29
July	-2.20	80-08-19	-1.90	80-08-27
August	-2.00	80-09-23	-1.10	80-09-26
September	-1.50	80-10-21	-1.60	80-10-28
October	-1.80	80-11-25	-1.90	80-11-28
November	-1.70	80-12-23	-1.70	80-12-30
December	-2.00	81-01-27	-3.00	81-01-28
1981				
January	-2.50	81-02-24	-5.40	81-02-27
February	-4.00	81-03-24	-3.20	81-03-27
March	-3.30	81-04-21	-0.50	81-04-28
April	-1.50	81-05-27	-3.50	81-05-28
May	-2.20	81-06-23	-3.40	81-06-26
June	-3.00	81-07-21	-3.10	81-07-28
July	-3.10	81-08-25	-1.50	81-08-27
August	-2.50	81-09-22	-5.60	81-09-28
September	-3.40	81-10-20	-2.60	81-10-28
October	-2.90	81-11-24	-5.30	81-11-30
November	-3.50	81-12-22	-4.40	81-12-29
December	-4,00	82-01-26	-1.60	82-01-28
1982				
January	-2.50	82-02-23	-5.10	82-02-26
February	-3.00	82-03-23	-1.20	82-03-26
March	-2.40	82-04-20	-2.60	82-04-27
April	-2.30	82-05-25	-0.30	82-05-26
May	-1.90	82-06-22	-3.30	82-06-25
June	-2.50	82-07-27	-3.40	82-07-28
July	-3.00	82-08-24	-2.40	82-08-26
August	-2.50	82-09-21	-7.10	82-09-27
September	-3.50	82-10-26	-4.20	82-10-27

Month	Forecast	Survey Date	Actual	Release Date
October	-4.00	82-11-23	-5.30	82-11-26
November	-4.90	82-12-21	-4.10	82-12-29
December	-4.50	83-01-25	-3.40	83-01-26
1983				
January	-3.50	83-02-23	-3.00	83-02-28
February	-3.50	83-03-22	-3.60	83-03-29
March	-3.50	83-04-26	-3.60	83-04-29
April	-4.00	83-0524	-4.60	83-05-27
May	-4.60	83-06-21	-6.90	83-06-28
June	-5.80	83-07-26	-5.00	83-07-29
July	-5.70	83-08-23	-6.40	83-08-29
August	-6.50	83-09-27	-7.20	83-09-28
September	-6.90	83-10-25	-5.80	83-10-28
October	-6.50	83-11-22	-9.00	83-11-29
November	-7.50	83-12-28	-7.40	83-12-29
December	-8.00	84-01-24	-6.30	84-01-27
1984				
January	-7.50	84-02-24	-9.50	84-02-29
February	-8.50	84-03-23	-10.10	84-03-29
March	-9.00	84-04-23	-10.30	84-04-27
April	-10.00	84-05-25	-12.20	84-05-30
May	-12.00	84-06-22	-8.80	84-06-28
June	-10.50	84-07-20	-8.90	84-07-27
July	-9.00	84-08-24	-14.10	84-08-29
August	-11.50	84-09-21	-9.90	84-09-28
September	-10.50	84-10-25	-12.70	84-10-31
October	-11.50	84-11-26	-9.20	84-11-30
November	-10.00	84-12-21	-9.90	84-12-28
December	-10.00	85-01-25	-8.20	85-01-30
1985				
January	-9.50	85-02-22	-10.30	85-02-28
February	-10.50	85-03-22	-11.50	85-03-28
March	-11.50	85-04-26	-11.10	85-04-30
April	-11.37	85-05-24	-11.90	85-05-31
May	-11.30	85-06-21	-12.70	85-06-28
June	-12.00	85-07-26	-13.40	85-07-30
July	-13.00	85-08-23	-10.50	85-08-30

Month	Forecast	Survey Date	Actual	Release Date
August	-12.50	85-09-20	-9.90	85-09-27
September	-12.00	85-10-25	-15.50	85-10-31
October	-12.00	85-11-22	-11.50	85-11-27
November	-12.00	85-12-20	-13.70	85-12-31
December	13.00	86-01-24	-17.40	86-01-30
1986				
January	-14.00	86-02-21	-16.50	86-02-28
February	-14.00	86-03-21	-12.50	86-03-27
March	-12.00	86-04-18	-14.50	86-04-30
April	-13.50	86-05-23	-12.10	86-05-30
May	-12.80	86-06-20	-14.20	86-06-27
June	-13.50	86-07-25	-14.20	86-07-30
July	-14.00	86-08-22	-18.00	86-08-29
August	-15.40	86-09-26	-13.30	86-09-30
September	-14.10	86-10-24	-12.60	86-10-30
October	-13.50	86-11-21	-12.10	86-11-26
November	-12.90	86-12-19	-19.20	86-12-31
December	-13.80	87-01-23	-10.70	87-01-30
1987				
January	-14.00	87-02-20	-14.80	87-02-27
February	-13.00	87-04-10	-15.10	87-04-14
March	-13.50	87-05-08	-13.60	87-05-14
April	-13.70	87-06-05	-13.30	87-06-12
May	-13.00	87-07-10	-14.40	87-07-15
June	-13.00	87-08-07	-15.70	87-08-14
July	-16.00	87-09-04	-16.50	87-09-11
August	-14.50	87-10-09	15.70	87-10-14
September	-14.70	87-11-06	-14.10	87-11-12
October	-14.60	87-12-04	-17.60	87-12-10
November	-15.00	88-01-08	-13.20	88-01-15
December	-13.80	88-02-05	-12.20	88-02-12
1988				
January	-13.20	88-03-11	-12.40	88-03-17
February	-11.50	88-04-08	-13.80	88-04-14
March	-12.40	88-05-13	-9.70	88-05-17
April	-12.00	88-06-03	-9.90	88-06-14
May	-11.00	88-07-08	-10.90	88-07-15

Month	Forecast	Survey Date	Actual	Release Date
Date June	-11.00	88-08-12	-12.50	88-08-16
July	-11.50	88-09-09	-9.50	88-09-14
August	-10.00	88-10-07	-10.60	88-10-13
September	-9.50	88-11-04	-9.00	88-11-16
October	-9.00	88-12-09	-8.90	88-12-14
November	-9.55	89-01-13	-11.00	89-01-18
December	-10.50	89-02-10	-10.20	89-02-17
1989				
January	-9.80	89-03-10	-9.50	89-03-15
February	-10.20	89-04-07	-10.50	89-04-14

Source: Money Market Service Inc.

Bibliography

Aggarwal, R. "Exchange Rates and Stock Prices: A Study of the U.S. Capital Markets under Floating Exchange Rates." *Akron Business and Economic Review*, 12, 2 (Fall, 1981), 7-12.

Alam, M. Shahid. *Government and Markets in Economic Development Strategies*, New York: Praeger Publishers, 1989.

Ang, James S. and Ahmed Ghallab. "The Impact of U.S. Devaluation on the Stock Prices of Multinational Corporation." *Journal of Business Research*, 4, 1 (February, 1976), 25-34.

Binder, J. J. "Measuring the Effects of Regulation with Stock Price Data." *Rand Journal of Economics*, 16 (1985a), 167-183.

Binder, J. J. "On the Use of the Multivariate Regression Model in Event Studies." *Journal of Accounting Research*, 23 (1985b) 370-383.

Binder, J. J. "The Sherman Antitrust Act and the Railraod Cartels." *Journal of Law and Economics*, 31 (1988), 370-383.

Brown, S. and J. Warner. "Measuring Security Price Poerformance." *Journal of Financial Economics* 8 (1980), 205-258.

Brown, S. and J. Warner. "Using Daily Stock Returns." *Journal of Financial Economics* 14 (1985), 3-31.

Bryant, Ralph C., Gerald Holtham, and Peter Hooper, ed. *External Deficits and the Dollar*, Washington D. C.: The Brookings Institutions, 1988.

Cornett, Marcia Millon and Hassan Tehranian. "An Examination of the Impact of the Garn-St. Gerwain Depository Institutions Act of 1982 on Commercial Banks and Saving and Loans," *The Journal of Finance*, 45, 1 (March 1990), 95-111.

Deravi, Keivan, Philip Gregorowic, and Charles E. Hegji. "Balance of Trade Announcements and Movements in Exchange Rates." *Southern Economic Journal*, 55, 2 (Oct. 1988), 279-287.

Dimson, E. "Risk Measurement When Shares Are Subject to Infrequent Trading." *Journal of Financial Economics*, 7, (1979), 197-226.

Dodd, P. and J. Warner. "On Corporate Governance." *Journal of Financial Economics*, 11 (1983), 401-438.

Fama, E., L. Fisher, M Jensen and R Roll. "The Adjustment of Stock Prices to New Information." *International Economic Review*, 10, 2 (Feb. 1969), 1-21.

Finger, J. Michael, H. Keith Hall, and Douglas R. Nelson. "The Political Economy of Administered Protection." *American Economic Review*, 72 (June 1982), 452-466.

Frank, Peter and Allan Young. "Stock Price Reaction of Multinational Firms to Exchange Realignments." *Financial Management*, 1, 4 (winter, 1972), 66-72.

Hardouvelis, Gidas A. "Economic News, Exchange Rates and Interest Rates." *Journal of International Money and Finance*, 7, 1 (March, 1988), 23-35.

Hardouvelis, Gikas A. "Macroeconomic Infornationa and Stock Prices." *Journal of Economics and Business*, 39 (1987), 131-140.

Hartigan, James, Screenivas Kamma, and Philip R. Perry. "The Value of Administered Protection: A Capital Market Approach." The *Review of Economics and Statistics*, 68, 4 (November, 1986), 610-617.

Hartigan, James, Screenivas Kamma, and, Philip R. Perry. "The Injury Determination Category and the Value of Relief from Dumping." *The Review of Economics and Statistics*, 71, 1 (February, 1989), 183-186.

Hartigan, James C. "The U.S. Tariff and Comparative Advantage: A Survey of Method." *Weltwietschafthches archiv*, 117 (March, 1981), 65-109.

Helkie, W. L. and P. Hooper. "An Empirical Analysis of the External Deficit, 1980-86." in *External Edficits and the Dollar*, ed. R. C. Bryant, G. Holtham and P. Hooper, Washington, D.C.: The Brookings Institution, 1988, 10-56.

Hilke, John C. and Philip B. Nelson. *U.S. International Competitiveness*, New York: Praeger Publishers, 1988.

Hogan, Ked, Michael Melvin, and Dan J. Roberts. "Trade Balance News and Exchange Rates: Is There a Policy Signal?." *Journal of International Money and Finance*, 10 (March, 1991), 590-599.

Hooper, P. and C. L. Mann. "Exchange Rate Pass-Through in the
1980's: the Case of U.S. Imports of Manufactures."
Brookings Papers on Economic Activity, 1, 1980, 297-329.

Hooper, Peter and Catherine L. Mann. *The Emergence and
Persistence of The U.S. External Inbalance, 1980-87,*
Princeton: Princeton University Press, 1989.

Kuo, Shirley W. Y. and John C. H. Fei, "Cause and Roles of Export
Expansion in the Republic of China." in *Foreign Trade and
Investment: Economic Development in the Newly
Industrialized Countries,* ed. Walter Galenson, Madison:
University of Wisconsin, 1985.

Lenway, Stefanie, Kathleen Ruhbein, and Laura Starks."The Impact of
Protectionism on Firm Wealth: the Experience of the Steel
Industry." *Southern Economic Journal,* 56, 4 (April, 1990),
1079-1093.

Patell, J. M. "Corporate Forecasts of Earnings Per Share and Stock
Price Behavior: Empirical Tests." *Journal of Accounting
Research*, Autumn 1976, 246-276.

Pearson, Charles S. *Free Trade, Fair Trade?,* Lanham: University
Press of America, Inc., 1989.

Prusa, Thomas J. "Why Are So Many Antidumping Petitions
Withdrawn?" *Journal of International Economics*, 33 (1992),
1-20.

Puffer, Marlene K."The International Reaction to U.S. Trade Deficit
Announcements." Working Paper, Rochester: University of
Rochester, 1990.

Rose, N. L. "The Increase of Regulatory Rents in the Motor Carrier
Industry." *Rand Journal of Economics*, 16 (1985), 299-318.

Samuelson, Paul A. "Proof that Property Anticipated Price Fluctuate
Randomly." *Industrial Management Review,* Spring 1965,
41-49.

Shapiro, Alan C. "Why the Trade Deficit Does Not Matter." *Journal
of Applied Corporate Finance,* 2, 1 (1989), 87-96.

Schipper, K. and R. Thompson. "The impact of merger-related
regulations on the share holders of acquiring firms." *Journal
of Accounting Research,* 21 (1983), 184-221.

Schole, M. and J. Williams. "Estimating Betas from Nonsynchronous
Data." *Journal of Financial Economics,* 5 (1977), 309-327.

Schwert, G. William. "Using Financial Data to Measure Effects of Regulation." *Journal of Law and Economics*, 24 (April 1981), 121-158.

Shiller, Robert J. " Do Stock Prices Move Much to Be Justified by Subsequent Changes in Dividends?" *The American Economic Review,* 71, 3 (June 1981), 421-436.

Smith, R. T., M. Bradley and G. Jarrell. "Studying Firm Specific Effects of Regulation with Stock Market Data: An Application to Oil Price Regulation." *Rand Journal of Economics*, 17 (1986), 467-489.

Soenen, Luc A. and Elizabeth S. Hennigar. "An Analysis of Exchange Rates and Stock Prices—The U.S. Experience Between 1980 and 1986." *Akron Business and Economic Review,* 19, 4 (Winter 1988), 7-16.

Theil, H. *Principles of Econometrics,* New York: Wiley, 1971.

Index

For Product Safety Concerns and Information please contact our EU
representative GPSR@taylorandfrancis.com Taylor & Francis Verlag GmbH,
Kaufingerstraße 24, 80331 München, Germany

Printed and bound by CPI Group (UK) Ltd, Croydon, CR0 4YY
08/05/2025
01864512-0001